D1601680

Beyond The Veil

Beyond The Veil

Lee Nelson

Volume Three

Copyright © 1990 by Cedar Fort, Incorporated

All rights reserved. This book or any part thereof may not be reproduced in any form whatsoever, whether by graphic, visual, electronic, filming microfilming, tape recording, or any other means, without the prior written permission of the author, except in the case of brief passages embodied in critical reviews and articles.

5 6 7 8 9 10

26 27 28 29 30 31 32 33 34

ISBN: 1-55517-064-1

Printed and distributed in the United States of America by:

CFI
Cedar Fort, Incorporated
925 North Main, Springville, UT 84663 801-489-4084

Lithographed in the United States of America

Publisher's Foreword

As we mentioned in the forewords of *Beyond the Veil, Volumes One and Two*, these projects have been supremely fulfilling. Nothing can come close to the experience of sitting across a table or on a sofa and having a person describe the physical features and demeanor of the Savior and other spiritual beings.

Also gratifying are the many, many letters that are received from people who have been benefitted by our efforts to make this kind of information available. We hope *Beyond the Veil, Volume Three* continues in that trend. We hope you find it enjoyable, informative, reassuring and comforting.

Like the accounts in *Volumes One and Two*, these also are extremely personal stories. They are private stories. We congratulate these individuals who have shared their experiences with us, for their courage. We believe wholeheartedly there will be many who will bless them in the hereafter for their spiritual strength.

As these volumes continue we fear greatly that somehow a manufactured story may get included. In practicality we have no way to prevent this. We cannot always tell when people are telling the truth. We do try very hard to feel the spirit of the story but, having not been beyond the veil ourselves, we have no premise other than spiritual feelings to use to edit these stories. We strongly suggest that you do the same thing.

These stories are not meant to be read and discussed from a doctrinal point of view, but used simply for whatever benefit may be individually appropriate. We specifically request that these stories not be passed on orally from friend to friend. This only invites inaccuracies and sensationalism. Please read and ponder these accounts in private and invite interested friends to do likewise.

Lyle V. Mortimer
Publisher

If, after reading these narratives, you are aware of a similar account, experienced by you or a loved one that would be an appropriate addition to the growing body of evidence that the human soul lives beyond the grave, we invite you to tell us about the account on cassette tape and send it to us for possible publication in a future volume of *Beyond the Veil*. Please include appropriate address and phone numbers in case we wish to obtain permission to publish the story.

Send to:

Beyond the Veil
Cedar Fort Incorporated
925 North Main Street
Springville, UT 84663

TABLE OF CONTENTS

Introduction

With over 65,000 copies of *Beyond the Veil*, *Volumes I, II and III* in print we receive many calls and letters from individuals who have been moved by the stories in these books. The most memorable responses come from people who perhaps received a copy of one of the books following the death of a loved one, and in reading the stories found comfort, hope, and a renewed confidence in a glorious afterlife for the lost loved one.

One of the most touching letters was from a lady in Chicago who lost two teenage sons in an automobile accident. She and her husband had not really been that active in the Church. After the death of her sons she called reading a copy of *Beyond the Veil* the "jump start" she needed. The couple had their sons sealed to them just five months after the accident.

Nothing can compare with the feelings of gratitude we feel when we receive letters like this. We are deeply appreciative for the opportunity just to be involved.

Some people, in discovering these beyond-the-veil experiences for the first time, have the feeling they have come upon something new and exciting. Actually, there is nothing new about such experiences, unless it is the number of books and movies now being written on the subject.

People have been having beyond-the-veil experiences as long as written history has been kept. King David talks about walking through the "valley of the shadow of death" (Psalms 23:4), possibly referring to the valley or tunnel so many people describe at the edge of death. The apostle Paul in New Testament times was more exact, saying, "I knew such a man, (whether in the body, or out of the body, I cannot tell...) he was caught up into paradise and heard unspeakable words, which it is not lawful for a man to utter" (II Corinthians 12:3-4).

In doing the research for my recently released biographical novel on Walkara, a Ute Indian chief, I uncovered what appeared to be a classic out-of-body experience. Walkara told the story to early trappers and later to the Mormons.

As a young man he went high into the Uinta Mountains in search of the Great Spirit called Towats. Walkara said his soul was troubled following the killing of some men in a neighboring tribe. He went to the mountains fasting, hoping for some kind of communication with Towats, possibly to receive a medicine dream.

After several days of prayer and meditation he describes leaving his body and traveling to the world of spirits where he was greeted by Towats, who instead of wearing buckskins, was dressed in flowing white robes. The Great Spirit gave Walkara a new name, and told him that someday a tribe of white people would settle in Ute lands, and when they did he was not to make war with them. Walkara assumed Towats was referring to the Spanish priests who had already visited the Utes, and promised to return. He didn't know anything about the Mormons at that time.

Walkara was happy in the world of spirits and did not want to return to mortal life, but Towats told him he must, so he did. Later when the Mormons arrived in Ute lands, Walkara led a band of two hundred well-armed warriors, and probably could have driven the white settlers out, but didn't because of the spiritual experience described above.

Sometimes people ask me if I have found anything supporting a belief in reincarnation in my research for the *Beyond the Veil* books. In fact, I was asked that question by a talk show host on KSL Radio. I was being interviewed on the air along with a woman who had written a book on after-life experiences. She said she had found a number of experiences supporting reincarnation. I can honestly say that in interviewing nearly a hundred people I have not found anything even hinting at reincarnation.

After reading a number of beyond-the-veil experiences associated with near-death, crisis situations, one might come to the conclusion that people involved with the death process have some kind of monopoly on penetrating to the other side of the veil. They may have an advantage over the rest of us when it comes to getting a glimpse of what lies beyond this mortal plane, but they certainly have no monopoly or exclusive right to seeing beyond death.

Down through the ages, including modern times, there are a number of ways in which people have successfully tried to penetrate the veil.

Involuntary physical stress is the catalyst to most of the beyond-the-veil experiences in these books. Fasting is a voluntary form of physical stress that worked for Walkara as well as for Jesus and many other religious leaders through the ages. The fasting is usually accompanied by very earnest prayer.

Some people have found objects very useful in penetrating the veil. Joseph Smith used and encouraged the use of seer stones. He translated much of the Book of Mormon by looking at a semi-transparent stone placed in the bottom of a hat. Others claim success with crystals, crystal balls, pendulums, even pocket knives.

Let me explain that one. A few years ago while driving through Provo, Utah, I saw a sign announcing a psychic fair at one of the local hotels. Not knowing what a psychic fair was, I decided to take a look.

Upon entering the fair I saw a number of people, mostly women, seated at individual tables facing the center of the hall. On the tables were crystals, decks of cards, ouija boards, books, pamphlets and other items. Several of the women were dressed like gypsies, but most were in normal every-day attire.

Some of these so-called psychics were busy talking to people, others just sitting and waiting.

I walked up to a young woman who didn't seem to be doing anything and asked her what her business was. She looked me in the eye and said that if I liked she would tell me some things about me that I didn't already know, perhaps some things about my future. When I asked her if there was a charge, she asked if $15 would be all right. I handed her the money and sat down across the table from her.

She asked if I had an object of some kind, that I usually carried close to my body, that she could hold. I thought of several items, finally settling on my pocket knife which I carried with me all the time, except when sleeping or taking showers.

She took the knife in her hand, carefully rubbing it between her thumb and forefinger. She asked if I was involved in the construction business. I said no.

"You are involved in some kind of construction project," she insisted. Impressed, but still skeptical, I told her I was in the middle of building a new house.

Next she told me I had a son who was or would be a good football player, and that I would be very proud of him. At the time my oldest son was playing on the Springville High School football team. By now she really had my attention.

She said there was a book I was supposed to read. I smiled, thinking she would now try to get more money out of me by selling me a book. I asked her if she had a book to sell. She surprised me by saying she had no books for sale, and she didn't even know the name of the book I was supposed to read. She closed her eyes, apparently in deep meditation.

"It's a black book with gold letters," she said after considerable thought. I told her that didn't help much, that there were millions of black books with gold letters. She closed her eyes and meditated some more.

"The first letter in the name is a P," she said. I asked her if it was a new book I would buy, or a used book I would borrow. I asked her where I could find the book.

She didn't think I would buy the book, but I would borrow it from a place or person with a name starting with the letter W. I asked her if the place might be the Whitmore Library in Salt Lake City. She said that might be the place, but she wasn't sure.

The next time I was in Salt Lake City, I stopped in at the Whitmore Library and browsed through the aisles looking for a black book with gold lettering. I didn't find anything beginning with the letter P.

A few days later I stopped in at Walt West's used bookstore in Provo. The psychic said the place were I found the book would start with a W. This place had two W's in its name.

No sooner had I strolled through the door than I saw a black book with gold lettering on the top shelf to my left. The first letter was a P, but I couldn't read the entire title because the book was on its side. I reached up and took it down. Wiping off the dust I read the title, "Progressive Wine Making."

Feeling more than a little foolish, I placed the book back on the shelf, but not before thumbing through the pages. It told about making wine, nothing more. I decided I would spend no more of my time in search of the book. If it was important that I read it, the book would have to find me. To date that has not happened.

It is obvious that bona fide beyond-the-veil experiences happen. They are of a nature, however, that is easily sensationalized. After my experience with the psychic fair I became more determined to try to find the difference between that experience and others that are uplifting and sincere.

Some tribes of native Americans claim the drug Peyote is a spiritual stimulant. Some people, too young and too foolish to know better, experiment with black magic, devil worship and ouija boards.

Several years ago I had an interview with a 16-year-old boy who had become involved in Satan worship and was trying to get out of it. He feared for his life because of some oaths he and his companions had made. I asked why he got into it in the first place, wanting to understand why anyone would want to be mixed up with the devil. He said he was promised he would become a rock star and popular with women—in exchange for his soul. At the time he thought the promised reward was worth the price.

The scriptures have numerous accounts of prophetic dreams as a means of receiving communications from beyond the veil. This must be a gift that some people have, and some don't.

About ten years ago I had a very real dream involving the death of one of my neighbors. The dream was very real. The man had a dangerous profession. I became quite concerned about the possibility that he might die. I debated a long time on whether or not I should tell him, eventually deciding I would not. Ten years later the man is still very much alive. While I think it would be desirable to have prophetic dreams, I'm sure glad, at least for my neighbor's sake, that I don't have that gift.

Once I read a book describing how some of your best ideas come from your subconscious mind in dreams. The book suggested that a note pad be kept by the bed at night, so when you wake up with a powerful idea you could write it down. If you didn't, you would probably forget it by morning. I put a pad and pen by my bed hoping to harvest wonderful ideas from my dream world, and hopefully tap the hidden resources of my subconscious mind.

I didn't have long to wait. A few nights later I had a dream involving an idea that would become the best selling novel with a Mormon theme of all time. The title of the upcoming book, which I would write, was given to me in my sleep, and when I awoke and sat up in bed, I could still remember it. I was so excited. I had no doubts but what the book would be a best-seller. I would begin working on it in the morning.

When I thought about writing the title on the note pad I hesitated, thinking I could never forget something so remarkable, so obvious, so important. Still, I forced myself to reach for the pad, then without turning on the light, wrote down the title of the best selling book I would write.

The next morning as I began to get out of bed, I suddenly remembered that during the night I had harvested from my dreams the title and subject matter for a fantastic book. For the life of me I could not remember what it was about. But I did remember the note pad. Picking it up, it took a minute to figure out the large scribbled message that I had written down without the benefit of light.

There was no mistaking what I had written down. The title of the new book was "Tarzan Goes to the Temple." I threw the note pad in the trash and have paid little attention to my dreams since.

There seems to be a spiritual awakening around the world. More people seem deeply interested in spiritual matters than ever before, at least more than they have been in my lifetime. Books on a wide range of spiritual subjects are selling like never before. The atheists have become mostly silent, and the governments founded on atheist theories are crumbling. In some countries Mormon missionaries are converting thousands, and they will convert many thousands more, perhaps millions, in the new countries just opening to the preaching of the gospel.

There is still plenty of wickedness in the world, but it's refreshing to see so many people searching for truth and guidance from beyond the veil. While some of the above mentioned methods may seem questionable—quick fixes and short cuts for those unwilling to pay the price of true religion—it seems good that an increasing number of people are looking towards the heavens to better their lives.

In all my searching, reading, interviewing, and exploring I keep coming back to what I knew all along. The humble prayer of faith, sometimes with fasting, followed by an intense effort to listen to that still, small voice is what works best. This, combined with a sincere effort to keep God's commandments and lighten the burdens of one's fellow brothers and sisters is still the best way to open the windows of heaven.

At one time I was seeking my own beyond-the-veil experience, even if it meant going through a near-death tragedy. I have repented of that desire. I still pray for guidance from beyond the veil, and find myself trying to listen to that still, small voice from time to time—but as for having my own beyond-the-veil experience I will pass, content to enjoy the experiences of others, like those following in this book.

When I began this project I didn't think there would be three volumes, but there are, possibly because there is so much variety in the numerous experiences people are having. Volume II was very different from Volume I, and as you read this volume you will find unique and different experiences worthy of publication, making this volume a welcome addition to what has already been published.

Some of the people I have interviewed pass through a tunnel. Others do not. Some find themselves in a beautiful room, others in scenic wooded areas. Some meet spirit persons in flowing white robes. Others see spirit people dressed in everyday work clothes. Some have pain in exiting and reentering bodies. Others do not.

I have come to the irrevocable conclusion that the spirit world beyond the veil is so different from this present world that we cannot understand it with the same assumptions and thinking we take for granted in understanding this world. As soon as I think I have reached a safe conclusion, I run into someone who has had an experience that makes me realize I still do not see the entire picture.

It seems everyone who has the opportunity to go there and return, sees the world beyond the veil a little differently depending on that person's experience and perceptions. Only by studying a large variety of experiences enjoyed by a wide range of people can we begin to understand and comprehend that beautiful world.

Volume One in this series starts the reader on the journey to understanding the world beyond the veil. *Volume II* deepens and broadens the reader's understanding. With new and sometimes very different experiences, *Volume Three* takes the reader even further, not only in understanding but in losing that fear many have of taking the journey we all must take, someday, beyond the veil.

Chapter One

An Ordinary Kid

by Sandy Greenley
with Radawna Michelle

Kendal was a typical nine-year-old most of the time. He loved to ride his bike and play on the trampoline.

He disliked anything to do with being clean or responsible, and WORK was a dirty word that he definitely liked to avoid. He loved bugs, animals and dirt; the dirtier he became, the happier he seemed to be.

School and homework created all kinds of trials and trauma for both Kendal and his family. Church and Sunday School were only for old people who needed something to do. Family prayer and scripture study were times to harass his family or sleep— whichever he decided on at that moment.

He thought children were born to love all people and to play. He never knew what the word stranger meant. Everyone was his friend, regardless of age, sex or race. He often called on teenagers, as well as adults to see if they wanted to play. Two of his best friends were 16 and 18 years old. They jumped on the trampoline and went for bike rides with him.

Another of his friends, Tressa, was in her thirties and they spent time together making animals out of balloons and learning how to be clowns. If he had had his way they would have spent time together every single day. He could never understand why she must spend time being a mother and wife. Friends were definitely supposed to come first.

This normal nine-year-old's life was changed for a moment on March 14, 1989. He entered my room at about 3:30 a.m. crying hysterically and trembling. He was so frightened he could hardly speak.

"What is the matter, Kendal?" I asked.

"Mommy, I have to decide who I want to live with, you or Heavenly Father, and I love you both so very much," he replied, his voice shaky.

"Why don't you just cuddle up in Mommy's arms and we'll worry about this later?" I replied, mustering all my motherly wisdom.

His small body continued to tremble for over an hour. I hugged, snuggled him and kept telling him how special he was—and that everything would be all right. I felt so peaceful inside, that I knew everything would be different once he settled down.

Nothing more was said. When morning arrived, life went on as usual.

Two days later, on March 16, the phone rang. It was the school, informing me that Kendal would be retained in the third grade if his grades and test scores did not improve. At this moment I was furious with Kendal and the school system. He was a very intelligent child, who just had trouble with motivation. He could tell you anything you wanted to know if he chose to. However he could also play dumb and not seem to know anything.

I spent the entire day crying and talking to learning centers, private schools and tutors. I wanted to make a good decision that would be beneficial to Kendal. When he came home from school, I asked him if he wanted to be held back and repeat the third grade the next year.

His answer didn't make any sense to me.

"It's okay, Mommy, I love you," he kept telling me.

What kind of answer was that supposed to be?

That evening we attended the pinewood derby, a cub scout racing event. The important thing about the derby was that each vehicle had to be homemade from a single block of wood.

Kendal and his dad, Dan, had made a special vehicle that year, an 18-wheel truck. Kendal was extremely proud of his truck. He told his father earlier when making it that it did not matter whether the truck won or lost because he had already been a winner. He got the car he wanted and his dad had helped him make it.

That night all of the day's crying and the noise and accompanying excitement of several races descended on me and my head began to pound. For just a moment I closed my eyes and took several deep breaths to relax and to ease the pain and stress.

While I relaxed, a scene entered my mind. I saw my son, Kendal as a young man, lying dead on a dirt road with a motorcycle on the ground beside him. I should have been upset, but a powerful feeling of peace and warmth surrounded my body. I simply and quietly told God that it was okay, that he was only nine now. About that time I was informed that Kendal was to race again, immediately bringing me out of my reverie.

The night following the derby Kendal was invited to go to K-Mart with a teenage friend. While at the store he spent his allowance in the machines at the front of the store, buying slime and friendship bracelets.

"Why don't you save your money and buy something really nice?" his friend asked.

"I don't have time," Kendal replied.

"What do you mean you don't have time?" Gary asked. "You're only nine. You have a whole lifetime."

Gary later told me Kendal looked at him as if he did not understand.

"Let's go get a Coke," Gary suggested, running his fingers affectionately through Kendal's hair. That was all Kendal had to hear to forget what was bothering him and get going again with life.

A week later, on March 23, on my way out the door to work, I reminded Kendal that the go-cart was off-limits. He loved to drive it around the front yard and I knew I wouldn't be home until late that evening. My neighbor, who could be depended upon to watch him in my absence, had left for a vacation and I wanted Kendal to leave the cart alone.

As Kendal kissed me good-bye he informed me that he was well aware of the rules and had every intention of following them.

"Besides," he said, "tomorrow is a school holiday and we are going to take the day off to do something fun as a family." He did not want to jeopardize his position and be left out or get into trouble.

At lunch that day Kendal approached Janet, one of the lunchroom ladies, and asked if he could have a grabber. A grabber was part of an incentive program started by the school to encourage better student behavior. To receive one a student had to have behaved in a manner the teacher thought worth rewarding. The student would in turn be given a chance to win a trip to Golf Land. Kendal knew his brother Donny loved grabbers.

Janet told Kendal that grabbers were only to be given to boys and girls who had done something special. She asked what he had done to earn one.

"I've been good," he said.

"How would I know that you've been good?" Janet asked. "I haven't seen you all day."

"Because I don't tell lies," Kendal replied, simply.

Janet felt a sudden softness in her heart towards the little boy and handed him the grabber—although she later could not really say why she gave in. His eyes lit up and he smiled a Kendal smile as he went about his business.

During art class that day Kendal was working on a necklace for Mothers' Day. He was very proud of it and took great interest in the project. He was excited about getting it finished, and when his teacher told the class that it was time to clean up and put things away, Kendal refused. After several minutes of frustration, his teacher finally decided it would be easier and faster to let him finish than to argue with him. He insisted on finishing the necklace although there was still six weeks until Mothers' Day.

When school was over Kendal was excited having a four-day weekend to look forward to. Kendal and his best friend, Brett, raced to the classroom where Brett's mother taught to see if they could go play together. After some degree of pleading they were on their way to Kendal's house for what they thought would be 30 minutes of fun and excitement.

No one was home so Kendal decided they should go for a spin in the go-cart. No need to stay in the yard, he reasoned, since no one was around to enforce the rules or to see that he honored previous commitments.

Kendal and Brett started the go-cart and headed straight for the orange grove that was two blocks away. When they arrived at the grove Kendal shut off the engine and began to look up at the sky.

"Isn't it beautiful, Brett?" he asked. "Look at all the animals and flowers. Aren't they beautiful?"

Brett's only answer was to remind Kendal that he only had a half-hour to play and he wanted to ride.

"In a minute, Brett. I just want to look at everything," Kendal said. "It is so beautiful, the people are so..."

Brett was frustrated. He folded his arms and began tapping his foot. Eventually Kendal got the message and said they could go home.

The cart would not start. This did not phase Kendal, however, as he immediately got out and flagged down a young man riding a motorcycle. Kendal asked for help in starting the go-cart.

The young man, Andy, was no stranger to Kendal, and pleasantly agreed to do so. After starting the cart, Andy left the grove. Kendal chose to go east, while Andy headed north. They were headed in different directions towards the same road.

When Andy reached the road he headed south. He saw the boys coming toward him on the edge of the road. The motorcycle and the go-cart were on the same side of the road. Andy's only thought was one of relief that the cart was still running and that they were having a fun time together.

In the second when the two vehicles were about to pass, Kendal made a sharp right turn in front of Andy. There was no chance to avoid the collision. The motorcycle cut the fiberglass go-cart in half.

Brett was thrown clear and sustained a broken arm and a few bumps and bruises. Andy had a broken foot, but was so occupied with Kendal, that he barely noticed the relative safety of Brett.

Andy worked frantically on Kendal, first to restore his breathing and then to stop the bleeding. Andy told me he was thinking the whole time, "I will just die if he dies."

Policemen, firemen and an air EVAC helicopter were called to the scene. Everyone worked to save Kendal's life. Eventually his breathing was restored and he was rushed to the hospital.

The neighborhood immediately began to work together. Donny, Kendal's older brother, was at the store with a friend. When he arrived home he was taken to a neighbor's house. Kendal's only sister, Debbie, was found waiting for a friend at school. She was taken to the hospital to be with her brother until the parents could be located.

A friend was waiting at our home for Dan. A telephone call was placed to me at work, but the call came too late. Reacting to an unknown inner stress I had been feeling, I had left work early.

I felt something was wrong, but even though the feeling was strong, it was vague, and I could not define the problem. I had been scheduled to help staff a seminar on self-awareness that evening, so I went there early, thinking that perhaps my uneasiness was associated with that.

When I walked in the door of the seminar hall I was told that I had received an emergency phone call and I was supposed to call my neighbors, Ellen or Sheri, as soon as possible.

My first thought was to wonder what had happened to Kendal. Although no one had specific information, I just knew the emergency had to do with my youngest child.

After talking to my neighbor, I placed a call to the emergency room at the hospital. The receptionist informed me that Kendal's condition was serious and that he was not expected to live. At the time of my call, Kendal was still in emergency surgery.

As I listened to this discouraging news, a small voice whispered in my head, "Let him go, he wants to go home. He is about his Heavenly Father's business."

Quietly, I told the nurse that our family had no insurance.

"Neither you nor the doctors are God," I said. "Please let him go in peace. Don't put him on life support." After informing the nurse I would come to the hospital as soon as possible, I hung up.

Upon entering the hospital my bishop was standing there, waiting patiently. He did not know how to express his feelings to the family. I offered a special prayer on Kendal's behalf then approached the bishop with tears in my eyes.

"He is meant to leave," I said, feeling peace in my heart. "I love him so, but he has to go. I know because the Spirit told me."

The look of relief on the bishop's face was unmistakable. He tried to hide it, but it was obvious he felt a burden was lifted. He and I then went to the hospital chapel where Debbie and many of the family's friends had already gathered.

I hugged my daughter and solemnly said to her, "No Debbie, I'm sorry. Kendal will be all right, but he is leaving us here and going on. He is not meant to live here with us any longer."

Debbie rebelled against the soft, final tones in my voice. I could not make her understand the need to let Kendal go peacefully.

Finally, Kendal came out of surgery and was placed in the intensive care unit. Two doctors came to the chapel to talk to the family. As they approached, my only question was whether or not he was on life support.

The doctors confirmed my fear and told me that life support was the only way to keep Kendal alive. They went on to explain all that they had done and how important the life support system was.

"You don't understand," I interrupted, impatiently. "There is nothing you can do to save his life. He is meant to go home. Please don't make him linger and suffer. You're not gods—and Heavenly

Father has called him home. Please, I beg you, let him go in peace."

The doctors explained that it was necessary for both parents to make that decision. I prayed that Dan would arrive quickly.

Debbie and I went to ICU to be near Kendal. When we reached the room, hospital personnel were scurrying around to get him settled. There was a palpable feeling of uneasiness in the air. I thought Kendal must be wondering how his family would handle the situation.

The room became quiet when the professionals left. Then it became peaceful as Debbie and I gazed at our dear Kendal. The doctors had said he was in a coma and could neither hear nor respond to his surroundings. Still, we felt sure that Kendal knew what was being said—that he was aware of the love and the feelings we had for him.

After Debbie left, I began to rub his feet and share my love and reminisce about old times. I believed Kendal shared this intimate time with me with everything but his consciousness. The love and warmth that was exchanged between the two of us was very, very real.

I was relieved to be able to express to Kendal that he could leave the earth—that his mother would let him go. I felt calm and peaceful as Kendal understood my love, my longing, and finally, my resolve to let him leave in peace.

Still, Kendal's spirit was troubled. One could almost sense the turmoil surrounding the small, battered body.

"Where is Daddy?" he seemed to want to cry out. "I love him so much and I want him to say goodbye before I leave. Where is he? He has to come quickly. This body is full of pain and I want to be free."

Dan was finally located and brought to the hospital. When he entered Kendal's room, he began demanding that his youngest son live. He told Kendal that he believed in miracles and one was about to be performed. His son was going to live, regardless of medical facts. His son was going to change medical history.

The spirit in the room altered. The peace diminished entirely and the pain could be felt more deeply than before.

I lovingly rubbed my husband's shoulders and reminded him of another situation where a person was kept alive through prayer. I pleaded with him to let our son go.

"Please let him be free," I begged, "He loves us enough to stay but do we love him enough to let him go?"

"I can't, I can't, I can't," he answered.

I told Dan to get a blessing or to pray, anything to get the strength to let our boy go.

"Think of Kendal," I pleaded. "He and God have made a decision. I know you are strong and I know this is tough, but please let Kendal be free."

Dan left the room, not knowing quite what to do. He loved his son and their life together was just beginning.

"Oh God," he prayed, "please help me to be strong and to let Thy will be done."

When Kendal's father returned I left the room so they could be alone. I knew Dan needed time with his son.

"My son, I love you so," he said. "You're very dear to me. You've taught me so much. I want you to know I know you're tough. If you decide to go, go quickly, please, and I will understand. If you linger I will know you want to stay. I'll help you. We'll work together no matter what it takes. I cannot bear to see you go. I'm leaving now. I'll come back in an hour or so to find what you have decided to do."

In a nearby hospital, at about the same time, Andy and his mother, Robin, were praying fervently for Kendal's life to be spared. Andy's mother had even called her church prayer circle to ask for their prayers on the little boy's behalf. It was a time when denomination did not matter, only the will of God.

After waiting for news of Kendal's condition, and after lengthy prayers, she heard a small voice say, "Let God's will be done."

Robin's inner turmoil was almost more than she could stand. She believed, faithfully, that she should pray that God's will be done—not that Kendal Greenley be allowed to live—and to let powers greater than those on earth decide the child's next step in his eternal journey. Still, how could she ever face

Kendal's family, knowing she had not prayed that his life be spared. The voice came to her again, "Let My will be done."

Robin then offered another prayer, that the Greenleys would have peace and understanding of God's will, whatever it might be. She prayed that God's will be done. When she was finished with her prayer, she felt a sense of inner peace. She knew that she had asked for the right things in her prayer this time.

Within five minutes of the time Dan left Kendal's room, and about the time Robin had felt the inner peace, Kendal decided to leave his body behind and begin a new life elsewhere. He was now free to go forward.

Kendal's departure brought new insights to the lives of those who loved him, along with the trials and tribulations which naturally accompanied his death.

One question that requires consideration is whether or not Kendal would have lived if his family and friends had not let him go. We believe he would have stayed alive on the earth. It was his choice. He knew the pain and grief his loved ones would go through in accepting his earthly absence, so the decision must have been difficult.

However, Kendal knew about a greater plan— the one designed by a loving and knowing Heavenly Father. We feel that it is important to let go of loved ones when the time comes for them to return to Heavenly Father's care. If they are not let go, earthly suffering can be prolonged and spiritual growth can be hindered.

As the funeral was planned, Kendal's spirit was near to let us know how things were to be done. Everyone felt a peace in their hearts when things were done correctly. A family friend made a special casket which was a beautiful work of art to honor the special young man Kendal had been.

After the funeral service, everyone was given a helium-filled balloon to send to Kendal by releasing them. The sky was soon filled with a beautiful bouquet of lavender, blue and white balloons. As they floated upward and onward, a great calm and peace was felt by all those in attendance.

The miracles associated with Kendal's last hours on earth were not the kind that shatter medical records. Kendal's miracles were those of love.

He left slime, from the machine at K-Mart, and a grabber that he had begged from Janet for his big brother, Donny. He left friendship bracelets for his special friends. He finished the Mothers' Day necklace for me and it is a gift I will treasure always.

We as a family learned that every situation in life provides an opportunity for growth, if one is open to learn. We learned the value of spending time together and sharing the words "I love you." We all realize that every moment in life is precious because no one knows how many more are left.

It is important for everyone to live their lives to minimize the guilt or pain that can be felt if a loved one leaves us behind on the earth.

Neighbors, friends, classmates and even strangers all worked together to pay for Kendal's medical expenses. The lessons, love and memories of Kendal will continue forever in those he touched.

Kendal was always loving towards others, regardless of the age, race, or status of the recipient of his affection. He set an example for all of us in that respect. He thoroughly enjoyed his free agency and let others know of the importance of making one's own choices. Kendal was always willing to pay the consequences of any decision, as long as he had the initial freedom to make the decision. He lived life to the fullest every minute he was alive.

Kendal Greenley is gone from earth now, but he is not gone from the minds and hearts of those he touched—and he touched many. Maybe Kendal wasn't such a typical nine-year-old after all.

Chapter Two

Resurrected Before My Eyes

as told by
Zeke Johnson,
November 5, 1954

I have been asked to relate an experience I had in 1908 or 1909 in San Juan County, Utah. I was just making a home in Blanding and the whole country there was covered with trees and sagebrush. I was working to clear the ground to plant a few acres of corn. We had five acres cleared and had started to plant the corn. I would plow open a furrow, then my boy would drop in the seeds. Last, I would cover the furrow by running the plow along the side of the row. While I was plowing on that piece of ground I discovered ancient houses, or the remains of them.

As I was moving along I noticed that my plow had turned over the skeleton of a small child. The skull and backbone were present, but most of the other bones were decayed and gone.

Immediately I stopped, though the plow had already passed the skeleton. I stepped aside and looked down, over the cross bar and between the plow handles. As I was looking at the little skeleton, wondering what to do about it, I noticed that the bones were beginning to wiggle and change positions, at the same time taking on a different color. A minute later I was looking at a complete little skeleton. It was perfect.

Then to my amazement I saw the inner parts of the natural body enter the skeleton—the entrails, organs, etc. I saw the flesh coming on, and I saw skin cover the body after the inner parts were complete.

A beautiful head of hair adorned the top of the head. The child was on its side with its back to me, so I wasn't able to discern its sex. But as it raised to its feet a beautiful robe came down over its left shoulder, and I saw it was a girl, maybe five to seven years old.

She looked up at me, and I looked at her, for perhaps a quarter of a minute. We just stared at each other, both of us smiling.

"Oh, you beautiful child," I said, reaching out to embrace her. Before I could touch her she disappeared.

That was all I saw, and I stood there wondering what it meant. Several minutes passed. My little boy was down at the end of the row wondering why I had stopped.

What I had seen was so mysterious that I decided not to tell anyone about it. I couldn't figure out why such a miraculous experience should happen to me.

I couldn't tell the story to anyone until finally one day I met a dear friend of mine, a stake patriarch named Wayne Redd, of Blanding. He stopped me on the street and said, "Zeke, you have had an experience on this mesa you won't tell. I want you to tell it to me."

I told him the entire story. From that time on he would often ask me to tell it in church meetings, at socials and in church conferences.

I wondered a lot about what had happened. It worried me for years. I wanted to know why a simple man like me—common and uneducated—was allowed to see such a marvelous manifestation of God's power. I prayed incessantly for an answer as to why I was privileged to see that resurrection.

One day as I was walking down to a field to hoe some corn, with my hoe over my shoulder, something told me to stop under the shade of a certain tree, and rest. The feeling was so strong that I decided to do it. As I sat down my prayers were answered. I was allowed to know why I had seen that resurrection.

When the child was buried there, it was either in a time of war with a different tribe and there was no time for a proper burial, or it was winter with the ground frozen too hard to dig a proper grave.

They buried the little girl as deep as they could, considering the circumstances. When it was done, the sorrowing mother, knew that with the grave so shallow, the first beast to come along would smell the body, dig up the child, and scatter the bones all over the flats.

There was a man present who told the mother to calm her sorrow. I believe he was a Nephite or Jaredite with priesthood power, because to comfort the mother he blessed the grave that if the little body was ever uncovered or disturbed the Lord would call it up immediately.

Since that time I have found great comfort, cheer, consolation and satisfaction in what happened. Sometimes I have such strong feelings in my heart and soul that I can't find words to express how grateful I am that I was the one blessed to uncover that little girl and witness her glorious resurrection.

Chapter Three

She Wore a Long, Flowing Gown

Lynn Lynes

I'm not sure where to begin this story, only that in the last two years, we have had many messages, inspirations and warnings from the Spirit, concerning our daughter.

Two years ago, Stephanie, age three at the time, was diagnosed with an inoperable brain tumor. She was given about six weeks to live. The Lord had other plans for her, allowing her to live nearly two years longer than the doctors expected. She died November 22, 1989, the day before Thanksgiving.

Early that morning, my husband, David, woke up realizing something was wrong with Stephanie. During the previous two weeks the tumor had progressed, and we felt that she was going downhill again. So many times Steffi had warned us that this day was coming. She knew, even though she was only seven years old.

David called me to the bedroom about 7:45 a.m. I had just gotten the other kids off to school, and was folding clothes in the kitchen. David's voice had a sense of urgency to it, so I dropped what I was doing to go upstairs, where David was holding Stephanie. She was limp and unconscious, and her breathing was irregular. She was gasping for breath.

"Oh, dear God, this is it," I whispered.

I felt a sense of despair, yet peaceful all at once. We had prayed continually throughout the previous two years that when the time came, she would go peacefully, at home, and in my arms. All I wanted to do now was hold my baby. I was grateful that she had slipped into unconsciousness while sleeping. And contrary to other times when Steffi had taken a turn for the worse, like when she had had a seizure, I did not panic, nor did I rush to the phone to call the doctor to ask what to do. The spirit was so strong, and I felt at peace with what would take place.

My greatest desire now, was simply to hold my baby as her spirit left this world, to return to her

Father in Heaven. I brought her into the world, and now I would see her gently out of the world.

At some point, I do recall feeling that Stephanie's spirit had left her body, but was present in the room. I looked upward, to speak to her, sensing that she was looking down upon us. I told her how much I loved her, and how proud I was of the way in which she carried her earthly burdens. I told her that she had many loved ones in the spirit world, and that her Father in Heaven loved her. I felt thankful that I had the privilege of being her mother. She had taught us so much and given us so much love.

David felt strongly that he should give Stephanie a blessing. He asked me if I was ready to let her go. How could a mother be asked that question? I was so torn. But I had the comforting strength to know that this is what our Father wanted, so it was what I wanted too. Yes, I was ready to let Stephanie go.

David gave his little girl one last father's blessing and commended her spirit to the Lord. She took several shallow breaths, then one last sigh, and peacefully slipped away.

How empty we felt, letting her spirit go. Yet the Savior's love brought peace and comfort into our home.

That same night I had difficulty sleeping. My heart ached. I knew Stephanie was where she should be, but I felt pain and loneliness that I've never felt before. My very soul wrenched with grief at the loss. I prayed that I could get some relief from this anguish, so I could sleep.

Then my eyes were opened to a most glorious sight. A place I think. Although I didn't actually see anything, I felt the presence of this place, and a beautiful young lady. She wore a long flowing gown, and just radiated with love and beauty and peace. She approached me and said, "I love you, Mother," and I felt her warm love embrace me. My Stephanie. She was released from her body and was now a beautiful mature spirit. Once again, I felt the peace of our Savior's love, and I was able to rest that night.

Chapter Four

Nobody Else Could See Him

by Fay Alvey

I was the third of seven children. We lived in Glendale, Utah about 38 miles from Kanab. The year I was twelve I was sick much of the winter. When my condition worsened in April, Dad called Dr. Norris in Kanab and described the symptoms. The doctor said it sounded like appendicitis.

My parents were deeply concerned because my older sister had died of appendicitis when she was my age. The only vehicle we had was a Model T pickup, so Dad made a temporary swap with the neighbors so we could use their touring car. We set out for Kanab, leaving my fourteen-year-old brother in charge of the family.

It didn't take the doctor long to diagnose me. My appendix had ruptured. There was no hospital in Kanab so they sent me on to Cedar City. I remember being very thirsty as we drove along, and Mother giving me water from a fruit jar.

We went straight to my father's brother's house in Cedar City and called the hospital from there. They said not to give me anything more to eat or drink, and to hurry me over to the old Iron County hospital.

When they operated, the gangrene had already set in, making it necessary for them to remove eight inches of my intestine and put in drain tubes. I seemed to come out of the operation all right, so father headed for home, leaving me and Mom at the hospital. She stayed there with me.

Complications set in. I caught pneumonia. The doctor said the appendicitis alone was enough to kill me. Now, with pneumonia too, he was really worried.

I remember lying in the bed, feeling pain and sickness at the same time. My mother was at my side. I remember looking at the cracks in the old walls. I had no desire to eat or drink.

Suddenly one of the cracks in the wall in front of me began to open up. Light from the widening crack filled the room. Inside the crack I could see stairs, leading upward.

I felt myself move away from my body towards the stairs. The pain was gone. The sickness was gone. I felt so good. I was on the stairs. It was easy to move up. But I looked back.

I could see my mother sitting by my body. My fingernails were black. My body wasn't moving. Mother called for the nurse. They were both leaning over me. A doctor entered the room and began giving me oxygen.

It wasn't long after that that two men in dark suits entered the room and began to give me a blessing. They were strangers. The one saying the prayer said the adversary was seeking to destroy me because of my ability to do good. He rebuked the adversary and promised me I would live to be a mother in Zion.

I knew I had to go back, but I didn't want to. Eventually I moved towards my body and willed myself to re-enter it. I'll never forget the horrible pain as I did so. It was awful.

The kids at school had heard I was dying, and began practicing a song to sing at my funeral. They made a wreath for me too. I think some of them were mildly disappointed when I came home alive and they didn't get to perform at the funeral.

A number of years later, in 1944, after I was married and had two children, my husband and I

were living in Escalante. He was working on the
maintenance crew on the mountain road. We were
not active in the church.

One day in December, while he was away, I
went down to the barn to milk the cow and feed the
pigs. I felt very sick, though I didn't know for sure
what was wrong. My head felt like it was two feet
above my body. I was suffering from a tubular
pregnancy but did not know it.

While feeding the pigs I passed out. My four-
year-old, LaVee, found me, and tried unsuccessfully
to get me up. She ran and got my seven-year-old,
Renae. I was conscious but couldn't get up. While
Renae was trying to help me we sent LaVee to the
telephone with orders to crank it five times, then
two—my father-in-law's phone number. She did it
and they came right down and got me into the house.

They called my doctor, Dr. Duggins, in
Panguitch, 70 miles away. He said he would come as
quickly as possible. He brought a young man with
him with my same blood type.

I remember lying on the couch in the living
room when the doctor arrived. There were a lot of
people in the room. I was surprised to see my father
who had died the year before, in September. I
remember wondering why nobody said anything
about him being there.

When neighbors came in to administer to me,
Dad was in the circle when they laid their hands on
my head for the blessing. Nobody else seemed to
notice him.

"Fay, you have to change your ways," Dad said to me when they finished the blessing. "You are not living your religion. You've got little kids and you've got to be more righteous."

After giving me blood, the doctor decided to take me to the hospital at Richfield for surgery. On the way, he looked into my eyes and said I was dead, that there would be no need to operate now. My heart had stopped beating.

Upon arrival at Richfield they decided to operate anyway, though my heart had stopped beating over four hours earlier. I could hear people saying I was dead, but I knew I was not. My spirit was still in my body.

Later when I thanked the doctor for saving my life, he said he didn't save my life because when we arrived in Richfield I was medically dead, and I had been in that condition for four or five hours. He said the only reason he could give for me still being alive was simply that my time was not yet up.

Upon recovering I remembered my father's words, and decided it was time to change my ways. My husband and I started going to church, and for the first time in years, I began accepting church callings.

Chapter Five

The Journey to the Bottom of the Hill

by Sally Taylor

I'm not really sure where to begin because this is the story of the end, not the beginning. But I think you need to know a few things about the past to understand. For instance, you need to know that Mother became a widow nearly fifty years ago when Harold, my father, was murdered by a hitchhiker. She moved with her five children—all of us eight or younger—back with her mother, Grandma Mary, and stayed there without remarrying until we all married and Grandma Mary died at 96. Mother returned to school to obtain two master's degrees and a doctorate while she worked to support us all.

You need to know that background to understand how much love Mother had for us and for Grandma Mary. We had a home full of love, hard work, education and sacrifice. We were close because Mother pulled us together in love and gentleness. But she was also a lot of other things: witty, bright, nonjudgmental, understanding, tolerant, and kind. We were not only proud of her, we knew that her love was the fulcrum of the family.

So it was understandable that when the long, downhill journey for Mother began, we would be there with her all the way. In the process we learned what it's like at the bottom of the hill—at death.

My mother's death had two dimensions: the physical side and the spiritual side. The physical side is easy to describe and document, but the spiritual side needs to be seen with different eyes.

Let me tell you about the physical side first. Her decline began with small strokes. It's hard to pinpoint exactly when they began. I noticed small things at first, like difficulty with driving—she would get lost and have near accidents. She burned pans on the stove. She became forgetful of very common things that she wouldn't have forgotten earlier—like taking her medication properly. Her sharp intellect was dimmed.

Finally, her inability to keep her financial and domestic affairs in order necessitated my taking over many things for her. When more serious illness came, we hired a companion and helper for her. Lenore was Mother's friend first and most importantly. She was also the chauffeur, the pill giver, the cook, the housekeeper, and the protector.

I won't detail the last illness which escalated the roller coaster ride to the bottom except to say that in October during her last stay in the hospital, she was given every test the doctors felt might be useful. There was no help. We brought her home to die.

As she became progressively more helpless, we often said in response to inquires about her, "She's going downhill." But we didn't know where the bottom of the hill was. I was often frightened and had nightmares about Mother's condition. Death seemed so terrible.

But it wasn't so terrible when we finally arrived together at those last moments. They were quite different from what we expected, though.

I think what helped the most with the physical side of death was the kind assistance and frank information given to us by Phyllis of Hospice. Phyllis came to Mother's home as we children gathered for a final goodbye. She told us that it was all right to cry. We would have many feelings, she said: anger, guilt, intense sorrow, depression, relief, pain, confusion, and grief. They were natural feelings. We should acknowledge and understand that they would come but would eventually fade.

She told us what the signs of death would be: 1) unusual coldness beginning in the extremities, 2) change in skin color, 3) change in breathing patterns, 4) death rattle in the throat, 5) final strong expulsion of air.

We were not to be overly concerned when Mother stopped eating. Her body was shutting down, Phyllis said. She didn't need the food. We weren't to force feed or bribe Mother with specially cooked food. She needed to let go. Mother's excessive sleeping was also a preparation.

Right at the moment of death and shortly thereafter, we were to be in no rush. She advised us to call the family around to give a final farewell. It was to be a sweet, loving time. She advised us to keep younger children away to avoid frightening them. We appreciated Phyllis' advice, and we remembered it when the difficult times came—beginning with Mother's reactions to food.

Mother's appetite left. She didn't want to eat for over a week. We took Phyllis's advice and encouraged her to drink a high-nutrition supplement called Ensure, but we didn't force food.

Her last meal was of Thanksgiving turkey. I came from the celebration at my home—my husband, children and grandchildren around me. The spot at the table where Mother always sat was filled with my eldest son. Mother had been bedfast for about six weeks. I went to Mother as soon as the dishes were cleared away.

"Mama, we just finished Thanksgiving dinner," I told her. "Couldn't I bring a plate over for you?"

"Yes," she said to me, "That sounds good."

I was back in a flash with plenty of her favorite dark meat, candied yams and jello with whipped cream. I also had some corn. I fed her slowly. She wouldn't eat the corn. I smiled.

"That's right, Mama," I said. "You've never liked corn, have you?"

"No," she said.

The next day she asked for some more turkey. It was her last meal.

The day of her death, November 27, Lenore was worried that Mother had been unable to drink. She had sucked water from some tiny mouth sponges, but that was all. I called the doctor. When he returned the call, he gave us three options: 1) We could take her to emergency, where she would have a food tube put down her throat and IV's in her arm for nourishment and fluid. That might keep her alive two or three months, he said. But in the end it would come down to the same thing we were facing now. 2) He could send a nurse to put in an IV for fluid. She might last two weeks, but she would gradually starve to death since she was not eating. 3) We could follow the course of "benign neglect," which meant we would give Mother all she could eat and drink by herself at her request. But we would basically let Mother go. He felt she would go within two or three days with this option.

It was a hard decision, one that I wouldn't make alone. Although all of my sisters and brother had been to see Mother in the previous two weeks, they had returned to their homes, so I called them all on the telephone for help in the decision.

We looked at the facts. In October the doctor had told us Mother's condition was irreversible, progressive, and terminal. Her quality of life was poor. She was bedfast, incontinent, and mentally confused. She had previously signed a living will stipulating that she didn't want to be kept alive by artificial means. The decision was unanimous—the third option.

I had a premonition that something was about to happen, so I prepared to stay the night with Mother. Janice, my oldest sister, was coming from Salt Lake City to join me—an hour drive, but Mother couldn't wait.

When the time actually came, Lenore and I sat on each side of the bed and watched the changes as Phyllis had detailed them. We were prepared for the natural signs, and we weren't frightened to see them come. What we didn't expect was the spiritual side to be so strong.

In the weeks before Mother's death, our spiritual selves felt other spirits gathering. They were loving spirits, comforting and soothing when they came. Mother often stared into space above her bed.

"What are you looking at, Lucile?" Lenore would ask.

"At the light," Mother would answer.

But the room was dark. We wondered if it was the same light Lenore once saw coming from Mother's room in the dead of night. It was a light that didn't come from lamps or fixtures. What did Mother see when she reached up with frail arms to the space above her bed?

"Take my hand," she said. "Help me up. I need to go home."

"Mother, I'm over here at your side," I said, able to see and hear with my physical eyes and ears only. "You are home. Where do you want to go?"

"If I'm a good girl, will you take me home?" she once asked.

"Oh Mama, you are always a good girl," I cried. "I'd take you home in a minute if I knew where home was."

She smiled at the empty air and watched something she never named. I realized she was now the one who knew where home was, not I.

As I mentioned, all of my sisters and my brother had been to see Mother within two weeks of her death. First my brother Jim and his wife came. Then my sisters, Joyce and Mary were "called" by unseen forces from long distances—calls which couldn't be ignored although the cost and time commitments were very awkward for them right then.

Somehow, Mother's need to say goodbye to her children, and their need to say goodbye to Mother was irresistible. It was a letting go—both for us and for Mother.

Each of us individually talked with Mother and assured her that everything was all right with us and with our families. Her spirit could be at peace. I also felt Grandma Mary's spirit with us—it was always strong. My sister Joyce felt Father's soft kiss. Lenore, Mary and Joyce all felt invisible hands drawing them to serve as they stayed in Mother's home.

The cats fled from the bedroom when the spirits came—except at the end when Maxwell, Mother's cat, sat alert in the chair beside the bed, his eyes wide, watching what we couldn't see. And then there were the voices.

Moments before her death as I sat watching Mother, I suddenly heard cheerful women's voices. Momentarily, I thought my sister Janice had come, and I wondered who she had brought with her. Then I knew it wasn't Janice. I asked Lenore if she heard the voices. She didn't. We stared at each other for a moment.

"Lucile, they're here for you," Lenore said, turning to Mother.

Mother shrugged her shoulders slightly, twice, as if her spirit was having a hard time leaving the body, then turned her head slightly and let out a deep breath. It was over—she had reached the bottom of the hill.

Lenore and I have talked frequently and at length about the voices. My physical self tries to rationalize them away—they were neighbors, I tell Lenore. But they were too near to be neighbors. The timbre and tone of their voices were too clear for me to deny—cheerful, excited, although I could make out no words.

"Remember," Lenore tells me, "I didn't hear them. It was only given to you." So my spiritual self has to admit, and cannot deny, what I heard.

As we expected, there have been many tears both before and after Mother's death. But some have been unexpected. Just after Mother's spirit left the body, Lenore asked if I wanted to be alone with Mother. I did.

I talked to Mother's unseen spirit and wept. And as I wept, a single tear came from Mother's eye and rolled down her cheek. Death had not robbed her of this last gift to me.

When Janice came, we called our families and the grown grandchildren who lived close. My husband and daughters were the first to come. They put their arms around me and we wept together. Then others came.

My husband mentioned the feeling of deep peace that had come to the house. There was truly a comforting presence and a reverence everyone felt.

Then all who had gathered stood holding hands around Mother's bed and said a goodbye prayer, thanking Mother for her goodness and love. And we wept. A similar circle had gathered when my sisters had all been there the previous week. That time, amid tears, we held hands in a lower room and asked for Mother's release.

Only after we had said a proper goodbye did we call the mortuary. When they came, they worked with graciousness and professionalism. As they took Mother out, Maxwell the cat followed the gurney and escaped into the night.

Through the period surrounding the funeral, we found ourselves weeping at odd times and for no apparent reason. Tears also came freely when we found a notebook as we sorted through Mother's papers. It contained tender letters Mother had written to my father beginning three months after his death and continuing for over thirty years. My sisters tell me that they are sweet, gentle letters about our growing up and of her great longing for him. I can't read them yet. The tears are still too close and the sorrow too tender.

Last weekend I found the record Lenore kept of Mother's medication and condition. On November 27 at 9:40 she wrote, "Lucile met Harold." I wept anew.

I once had a recurring daydream that I inherited a large mansion—a castle or manor house—and drifted to sleep night after night contemplating going through vast treasures of silver and linen, of paintings and antiques. The reality of inheritance is sadness. Each cracked bowl and valueless knickknack brings swarms of memories that are bittersweet because they each remind you of what was and is no more. There is nothing, no matter what the monetary value, that makes up for the loss.

Looking back over not only the last few difficult months, but also over the years, I understand why I will never completely let go of Mother's memory. I was many people to Mother through those years of our love: her baby, her little girl, her close friend and companion, her confidante, her grown daughter who lived around the corner and was a central part of her life, her caretaker, her daughter-turned-mother, and now, the keeper of her memories, the repository of her stories.

Sometimes these selves blend into indistinct patterns like a watercolor left out in the rain. Sometimes I wanted to go back to being her little girl. At the end I only wanted my friend back. Now as her memories are all that are left, these selves blend, and separate, and blend again.

She is so much a part of me that my days are full of wanting to turn to her, yet having to turn away. She can't see my new dress, my new haircut. I can't tell her about the book I'm reading, or take her to lunch as we did every day for nearly ten years. I don't call to see how she is feeling or stop by after church to sit by her sickbed. The hardest of all was to take her out of my prayers.

Chapter Six

My Spirit was being Pulled from My Body

When I was nine years old I remember getting a horrible pain in my side. I began throwing up. When the doctor saw me he said I had appendicitis and rushed me to the hospital in Bennington, Vermont.

I remember waiting what seemed like a long time in the emergency room, being taken to my room, then to the operating room. I was on a green table. They had taken off my clothes and covered me with a sheet.

I remember feeling embarrassed when the nurse pulled down the sheet. Then I didn't care, I felt so terrible. I looked around the room at the tools and machines. I was afraid. The doctors began to work on me.

I looked straight up into the air, thinking my time had come.

Suddenly my body was tingling all over. It felt like someone was pulling on me. My spirit began to come out of my body, starting at the head then working down to my feet. I remember slowly rising above my body, then turning over so I could look down at myself. The pain and sickness were gone. I felt happy. I felt very good.

I could see the open incision where the doctors had started to operate on me. The doctors were moving about quickly. One began to pound on my chest. A nurse was crying.

I turned to an upright position and returned to the floor. I walked behind the doctors, watching them work on me.

"Come to me," someone called to me. I looked across the room where a man in a long white robe was beckoning to me. I walked over to him.

"Look," he said, pointing to my body on the operating table.

"What are they doing?" I asked.

"Trying to revive you," he said.

"What's that?" I asked, seeing the doctors were trying to cover my face with something.

"An oxygen mask," he said. Then taking me by the hand he said he was taking me home. I refused to go with him.

"What's wrong?" he asked.

"I want to stay," I said.

"Why?" he asked.

"Mother needs me," I said. I was concerned about my brothers too. The man told me some things about my mother, and that she didn't mean to hurt me when she became angry, that she did love me very much.

"Do you want to see somebody?" the man asked.

"Yes," I said.

He took me by the hand and led me to another man who was sitting in a chair. He was wearing a white robe too. The man I was with picked me up and handed me to the man in the chair, who held me and talked to me. I can't remember the words, but I can remember the love I felt. I knew he loved me with a perfect love. He had white hair, but I couldn't see his face.

Eventually he handed me back to the messenger who took me by the hand and led me away.

"Look," he said, pointing to two young men in dark suits. He said someday I would join the

Lord's church, and these two young men would teach me the gospel.

"Be good," were the messenger's last words as he led me back to the operating table.

The next thing I remember was seeing my mother come into my room the following morning. When I told her I saw the doctors placing the oxygen mask over my face, she told me I hadn't seen any such thing. I didn't say any more. Later I heard one of the doctors telling my father I had almost died.

I pushed the experience to the back of my mind, never discussing it with anyone. When I was 20 I met two young missionaries. It took several weeks to realize they were the same young men the messenger had shown me in the operating room.

I joined the church, and was later told in a patriarchal blessing I had been give a witness to my soul of the truthfulness of the gospel, that I had earned this in the pre-earth life.

Chapter Seven

A Positive Knowledge

by Juanita Brooks,
As told in a letter of consolation to a Brother and
Sister Esplin who had just lost their son, Max.

September 11, 1939.

Dear Brother and Sister Esplin:
When I heard of your great loss, I felt that I
must drop everything else and come out. I knew
there would be little that I could do when I got there,

but I did want to let you know of my sincere sympathy. But I did not get word of the accident until the morning of the services, and too late to get anyone to stay with my babies before Brother Schmutz left at nine o'clock. So I must use this poor way of substituting.

When death comes at the end of a long and useful life, it is beautiful. When it comes as release from hopeless suffering, it is a blessed release. But when it snatches one in the full flower of splendid young manhood, it is hard to understand. We cannot understand. If we try to get at the great "WHY" behind it, if we blame ourselves and think that if we had only done some things differently it might not have happened, we only add suffering to our sorrow. We must accept and trust, knowing that we cannot understand the purposes of God.

Dear Sister Esplin, I know your faith. In all my life I have never seen its equal. I am sure that your husband also has faith in the goodness of Him that doeth all things well. I know that you will receive comfort from that source, and assurance that all is right with Max, that he is well and happy, and in a condition to advance and accomplish things that he might not have had here. Be glad that his passing was swift and painless. He merely stepped out of this body into a new and beautiful life.

I am tempted to tell you an experience of my own which has changed my whole attitude toward our passing from this life. I have told it before, especially immediately after it happened, and even wrote it then, so that I would not forget it.

It happened when I first came here to teach. I was not well, and I gave myself so completely to my work that I was completely exhausted every night. One evening I climbed the hill to my home, and was so tired that I went right to my bedroom and lay on the bed on my back.

Soon I had the sensation of being away from myself. Without any pain whatever, I was just separate from my body. I could see it, and wished that my mouth were closed. But I just kept thinking, "How strange! So this is what it is like to be dead!" I remember how I wondered at it and how surprised it made me.

"Francis will soon be here and find me, and he will call the folks," (I thought,) and so my mind ran on.

Then suddenly, without the lapse of any time, I was at my father's home in Bunkerville. I thought how sad (it was) that two who had had so many children should be there alone now. They were in the living room; there was a fire in the fireplace, and mother was stirring some mush in a saucepan over the coals. The house was so large and cold that they had not come into the kitchen to make a fire, and Daddy liked mush for his supper.

He was shaking some cream in a two-quart jar, because their one cow did not give enough to use the big churn. And he was telling her how one of the horses had got another into the manger and was kicking it.

"The old fool would have killed him if I had not gone out," he said.

I remember little things like the fact that the lamp wick was not even and the flame was blacking the chimney a little on one side, and some ashes from the big log fell into the mush and when mother tried to get them out Daddy said, "What won't fatten will fill." I'm telling you all this to make you see how very real it all was to me.

And then in another flash, I was back in my bedroom in St. George, and on the bed, and able to move. But through it all I was filled with wonder, and kept saying, "So this is what it is like to be dead. I didn't think it would be like this."

And when I was looking at my parents in Bunkerville, I thought, "Soon they will get the word that I am dead." I even wondered if the funeral would be in St. George or Bunkerville.

Well, Francis came just after I had come to and turned over. I told him all about it right then. That was Friday night, and on Sunday we went home to visit, and I told my folks, and every word of their conversation was real, even to the slang word mother used when the cinders fell in the mush, the churning, the horse in the manger, the smoking lamp, and all.

Dear friends, I didn't expect to write this when I started. I don't know why, except that the experience took the horror out of death for me. It gave me the positive knowledge that we are alive and conscious and intelligent after. I think that the Lord probably had things for me to do here, or I never would have come back.

This is an awkward expression of what I would say to you, but I do want you to know that you have my love and sympathy, and that I am sure all is well with your son. And I want you, Lucy, to know that more than any person I have ever met, you have been an inspiration to me.

The Lord bless you both, as I am sure he will.

Sincerely,
Juanita Brooks

Chapter Eight

I Went to See Joseph

by Brigham Young

Journal entry, February 23, 1847

I met with the brethren of the twelve in the historian's office. (A) conversation ensued relative to emigration westward. I related the following dream.

While sick and asleep about noonday on the 17th inst., I dreamed that I went to (see) Joseph. He looked perfectly natural, sitting with his feet on the lower round of his chair. I took hold of his right hand and kissed him many times, and said to him: "Why is it that we cannot be together as we used to be(?) You have been from us a long time, and we want your society and I do not like to be separated from you."

Joseph, rising from the chair and looking at me with his usual, earnest expression and pleasing countenance replied, "It is all right."

I said, "I do not like to be away from you."

Joseph said, "It is all right; we cannot be together yet, we shall be by and by; but you will have to do without me a while, and then we shall be together again."

I then discovered there was a hand rail between us, Joseph stood by a window and to the southwest of him it was very light. I was in the twilight and to the north of me it was very dark.

I said, "Brother Joseph, the brethren you know well, better than I do; you raised them up, and brought the priesthood to us. The brethren have a great anxiety to understand the law of adoption or sealing principles and if you have a word of counsel for me I should be glad to receive it."

Joseph stepped toward me, and looking very earnestly, yet pleasantly said, "Tell the people to be humble and faithful, and be sure to keep the spirit of the Lord and it will lead them right. Be careful and not turn away the small, still voice, it will teach you what to do and where to go; it will yield the fruits of the kingdom.

Tell the brethren to keep their hearts open to conviction, so that when the Holy Ghost comes to them, their hearts will be ready to receive it. They can tell the spirit of the Lord from all other spirits, it will whisper peace and joy to their souls; it will take malice, hatred, strife and all evil from their hearts; and their whole desire will be to do good, bring forth righteousness and build up the kingdom of God. Tell the brethren if they will follow the spirit of the Lord they will go right. Be sure to tell the people to keep the spirit of the Lord; and if they will, they will find themselves just as they were organized by our Father in Heaven before they came into the world. Our Father in Heaven organized the human family, but they are all disorganized and in great confusion."

Joseph then showed me the pattern, how they were in the beginning. This I cannot describe, but I saw it, and saw where the priesthood had been taken from the earth and how it must be joined together, so that there would be a perfect chain from Father Adam to his latest posterity. Joseph again said, "Tell the people to be sure to keep the spirit of the Lord and follow it, and it will lead them just right."

Chapter Nine

A Gentle Squeeze

by Dr. Alan Gomez

In 1989, after the first volume of Beyond the Veil was published, a 94-year-old woman named Angie Turpin made an appointment to see me at my medical practice in Provo. I specialize in foot problems and in a typical day's time see many older people.

I remember hearing Angie in the reception area, insisting she come into the examination room alone, that her daughter remain outside. She got her way, entered the room alone, seated herself in a chair, and waited for me to enter the room.

"This was written by Mormons for Mormons," she said when I entered the room. She waved a copy of Beyond the Veil at me.

"I just want you to know that Catholics have these kinds of experiences too," she continued.

"I don't have any problem with that," I responded.

Angie told me how she was the youngest in a family of eight children. They lived in the Enterprise area of Southern Utah. When she was eight years old her father was very ill and confined to his bed for a long time. For months he was unable to talk, except for occasional groans.

He was in a bedroom off the kitchen where his wife could keep an eye on him. At meal times she would sit at the head of the table where she could see into his room.

One Sunday as the mother and children were seated around the table for supper, the father suddenly started talking. Everyone rushed into the bedroom hoping he had taken a turn for the better.

The man was kneeling in the middle of the bed. As the mother and children watched they realized their father was not talking to them, but to unseen persons in front of him. As he continued to talk, addressing his spirit visitors by name, it became apparent he was talking to a brother, a former best friend, and his mother—all of whom had died.

"If you'll take me, I'll lie back down," were his last words. He smiled, rolled onto his back, and died.

When Angie finished her story, I asked what I could help her with, assuming she had a medical reason for making an appointment to see me. She said there was nothing wrong with her, that she had made the appointment to tell me about her father—that she wanted me to know that Mormons weren't the only ones who received visitors from beyond the veil.

About this same time another woman came into my office wanting to clear up a bill for her mother who had recently passed away. She also had a story to tell me about a woman who loved her foot doctor.

The mother's name was Violet Finocchioli. She was from Gary, Indiana and had worked for many years in a General Motors assembly plant. She had won awards for her productivity. She used the colorful, sometimes crude, language of a factory worker, and those who knew her said she could drink most men under the table. She was also a heavy smoker, and as a result had a severe case of emphysema. Because of smoking related circulation problems she had infection in her feet and had gangrene in one of her big toes.

Violet's daughter brought her out to Provo and made arrangements for me to look at the feet. I convinced her to cut back on her smoking—and that, combined with the treatment, enabled us to cure the gangrene problem. Though Violet was a rough talker, she was consistent and pleasant in her conversations, and we became good friends. She returned to Indiana.

Her emphysema continued to worsen until she became dependent on supplementary oxygen. Eventually her daughter brought her back to Provo and arranged for her to stay in the East Lake Care Center across the street from the Utah Valley Medical Center.

She called me her "lovely foot doctor" the first time I went to see her. Soon she was on a respirator and couldn't talk at all. The last time I visited her, after trimming her toe nails and checking her feet I gave one of her feet a gentle squeeze.

"Thanks," she said, feebly. I think that was her last word. She died the next evening.

When her daughter came in to see me about the bill she said that on the evening after my last visit she and her brother visited Violet. They were seated in her room. Violet was sitting up in bed, hardly breathing. They were in her room a long time thinking she wouldn't last long, and they wanted to be there when she passed on.

Suddenly Violet's eyes opened wide. She raised her hands, the palms facing outward as if she were pushing someone away from her, or preventing someone from coming to her. She was shaking her head sideways indicating she didn't want any part of what was about to happen. Then she looked in another direction, still shaking her head to indicate a negative response to whatever was being asked of her. There was fear in her face.

Suddenly Violet looked in another direction and began to smile as if she recognized someone. Her palms turned inward as she brought them to her body, almost like she was trying to embrace someone, or at least invite them to come closer. Her head nodded up

and down indicating an affirmative answer. The next
minute she was gone.

Chapter Ten

Some Kind of Mistake

by Ned Larson

In July of 1976, about four or five in the afternoon, my heart attack began. I was loading short railroad ties into the back of my pickup on some property where we ran cattle twenty miles up Spanish Fork Canyon, east of Spanish Fork, Utah. I was about 17 miles from my home in Mapleton.

The attack began with sharp pains behind both of my collar bones, just below the base of the neck. After four or five minutes my chest felt like it was being squeezed, under some kind of pressure.

I decided to drive up to my ranch where I could lie on the grass under the shade of a tree until the pain and discomfort went away. It hadn't yet occurred to me that I was having a heart attack.

I was driving towards the ranch when something told me I had better get out of the canyon while I still could. Upon reaching the highway, instead of turning towards the ranch, I headed straight for home.

I hadn't gone more than a block when I felt a numbness pouring from the neck and chest area into my arms. It was a smooth sensation, like someone pouring water. At the same time I felt the numbness moving up my neck into my head. The fight was on to see if I could make it home.

I told myself I wasn't going to go any faster than forty miles per hour in the event I got in an accident. I set the speed control at 40 mph so I could forget about keeping my foot on the accelerator.

I began to black out, at least partially. I kept repeating to myself that if I could just make the straight-away east of Thistle I would be all right. When I made that I told myself if I could make it to the Thistle rock I would be OK. Next the old D.O.L. gas station, and then Castilla hot springs. I was becoming increasingly fuzzy in the head.

By the time I reached the Covered Bridge Canyon turnoff I was mostly unconscious. I decided I had better pull off the road before I hurt someone. This was before the road was widened, so I had nowhere to go but off the oil onto the sloping shoulder.

I got out of the truck and sat down on the ground by the right rear tire. I was trying desperately to find a position where the pain would be relieved. I tried stretching out on the ground, first on one side, then the other, then on my back, then over on my belly. I tried lying down with my head uphill, then downhill. I even stood up again.

Nothing seemed to help. The pain kept getting worse. By this time I had started passing out, but always regained consciousness.

Finally I went around to the front of the truck and pulled myself up on my knees with the help of the bumper, and stood up.

"Lord," I said, "If I am going to die, and this is how it is going to happen, I am not afraid. I can't ask for favors because the life I have lived has not been as it should be."

"Mother, Dad," I said, continuing, "if you are there, answer and let me know. If I could talk to either one of you it would help me."

For the first time in my life I felt like I had come from an egg or from under a rock. There was no feeling of anything, no ties to Mother or Dad, or my lineage.

I was facing west across the river looking at the maples on the side of the hill. Suddenly I felt myself

rising in the air above the truck, looking down. I
ascended into the sky, looking west, but traveling
east. All at once the road was gone, so were the
railroad tracks. Where the highway and railroad
tracks had been there were trees. It was as if I had
gone back in time a hundred, or perhaps a thousand
years. There were no signs of man.

"This can't be," I said to myself. "I have traveled
this canyon for years. There's got to be a mark, a
trail, or something."

Then as suddenly as I had left, I was back in my
body. The pain was bad. I crawled back to the right
rear tire, tried to sit up, then passed out. Again I was
out of my body, looking down at it. My feet were uphill
towards the truck, my head downhill towards the
gutter. I was on my left side. A fly was flying around
my face. I wanted to slap at it.

Suddenly I began moving up the mountain,
suspended in air, like I was flying Buck Rogers style.
It seemed I was traveling 20 to 25 miles per hour.
Each time I drifted into unconsciousness I was in a
light fog.

The air smelled like fresh rain. The branches on
the trees were wet. I thought it strange that no leaves
were on the trees. It was July, or was it?

As I was speeding up the mountain I suddenly
felt the presence of someone else. At the same time I
was getting too close to the trees.

"Look out," I said, "we're going to crash and get
hurt in those limbs." We plowed into the trees. I
threw up my hands to protect my face, but I couldn't

feel any of the limbs hitting me. Finally, I took my hands down as tree tops flashed by on both sides of me. Nothing seemed to hurt me.

Then I found myself in some kind of strange cubicle, or it seemed so because it was totally quiet and I couldn't feel the air against me as I ascended up the mountain. The space I was in was three steps in one direction and four in the other. I could see the surrounding countryside in all directions. It was as if I was in a different dimension or time zone. It seemed my space or cubicle was made of glass and closed in.

I was standing in the front, in the northeast corner, and it seemed someone else was in the southwest corner at the rear. I took a quick glance back to see who it was, but received the distinct impression that I wasn't supposed to look. I tried to strike up a conversation, but after two or three short attempts, I felt I wasn't supposed to do that either.

Earlier, it had been very painful to breathe. Now as I attempted to breathe, I realized I didn't have to. All the pain was gone.

We were gliding up the mountain. Then all of a sudden I was back in my body sitting by the right hind wheel of my pickup. The pain was terrible.

"Lord," I prayed. "I'm going to ask something, not for me but for my wife. She's been a good woman all her life. If she comes up here in the middle of the night looking for me, and sees my truck over here, and tries to turn around, she might get in an accident and hurt or kill herself. Or someone else might. So if it's at all possible I would like to get out of the canyon so she won't have to come looking for me."

As I sat there, I could hear cars passing on the highway. I could hear the wind blowing up the canyon. I remember thinking how quiet it was, then thinking how stupid I was to think that.

Then I was in the enclosure again, high above the mountains, traveling very fast. It seemed I was a mile or two above the ground. I remember thinking that if I could get lower I could see better. Then, like, a flash I was traveling about a half mile above the mountains.

As I traveled along I remember seeing a light at the end of a large hole, which looked something like an irrigation culvert, but much bigger. I was being sucked towards it, and thought I was going to enter it—an endless vastness of forever.

I was almost into the tunnel when it suddenly disappeared, and I found myself in a bluish blackness. Everything around me was bluish black. It was like I was in a river. If I could get to the bank I could grab onto something, but there was nothing to grab onto. Everywhere was a bluish blackness.

Then I was moving along. In the distance I could see a light, similar to about an eighth moon, upside down. It was a long way away.

Then I had the strangest sensation, like my flesh was disintegrating and falling off my upper arms, then all over. It seemed my very being was discharging into nothingness.

Then I was back in my body, coming back and forth between consciousness and unconsciousness.

Once in a while I could smell the moist, damp air, and feel the water dripping off the twigs and small branches, like after a storm in the fall when the leaves are off the trees, but every time I returned to consciousness I could see the leaves on the trees, and feel the hot and dry July air. I was groggy, and totally unaware of the passing of time.

Then I heard music. I looked around and couldn't see anything, then began to pass out again, but the music brought me around. It sounded like it was coming from the front of the truck. I couldn't see anything from where I was sitting.

Closing my eyes again, I could hear the music clearer. Opening my eyes, I looked behind the truck, then under it. Nothing. Then I crawled to the front of the truck. Still I couldn't see anything, so I crawled back to the right rear tire. Leaning against the tire, I could hear the music again. It sounded like it was coming through a four-inch pipe or hose into my left ear.

I began crawling again, looking for the source of the music, but couldn't find a thing. I made my way around to the left front of the truck, and managed to get up on one knee. As I looked around the music stopped.

I was just dropping to all fours again when a movement caught my eye. Looking up the canyon, and down off the road, I saw a boy. When he saw me he ducked out of sight. Then two heads appeared, two boys.

I tried to speak, but I don't think any sound was coming out. The wind was blowing too, making a lot of noise. I motioned for the boys to come over to me. They ducked out of sight. I suppose they thought I was probably drunk, and with all my rolling around in the dirt, plus my unshaven face I probably didn't look very good either. I dropped back to my hands and knees and began crawling back to my place by the right rear wheel.

"Hello there. What's wrong?" someone asked. I looked up to see a man walking towards me. I waited until he was near then told him I had a terrible pain in my back and chest. I asked if I could hire him to take me home. I told him where I lived. He told me to give him a minute to explain to the other vehicle in his party what was happening. A few minutes later we were on our way down the canyon.

I looked up in the sky and quietly said, "Thank you very much." I fought desperately to stay awake, or conscious, so I could continue to give the driver directions to my home. I kept drifting into unconsciousness, but every time he had a question, I seemed to be able to rally enough to give him the answer he needed.

When we arrived home I had him pull onto my brother's lawn across the street, and honk the horn. The man seemed hesitant, but did as I asked.

My brother, Clyde, came around the corner of the house, and when he saw me, he said I had had a heart attack. That was the first time I realized what had happened to me. Clyde backed out his car and pulled me into the back seat with him while the fellow from the other car drove us to the hospital.

I stopped fighting to remain conscious. Finally, I could relax, knowing Clyde would take over. The next three or four days were blank.

I was in the hospital three weeks. During that time I kept reliving what had happened during the heart attack. Some of the events came back to me at that time, but it was early the following winter that I remembered the rest of what happened. I was home reading a biography about John Taylor, the third president of the LDS Church, and came to a passage where he was quoted as saying something like, "The veil is so thin that if our eyes were adjusted properly we could see right through it." As I read this passage some of the things I had experienced and more of the events of that day began coming back to me. Six years later I wrote everything in my journal.

Sometimes I wonder why I kept going back and forth between consciousness and the other dimension, and why the tunnel with the light at the other end suddenly disappeared just as I was about to enter it. And what about that moment when the flesh was falling off my arm? How near death was I?

I can't help but wonder that maybe the power on the other side had made a mistake, and my time was not then or they didn't have a place prepared for me.

Whatever the situation was, they solved or avoided the problem by letting me return, and I'm glad they did. So is my wife.

Chapter Eleven

I Could See the Buttons

by Fern Hicks

It was a beautiful spring day in 1987. I was on the sidewalk in front of my home in Pleasant Grove, Utah. I had gone outside to inspect some repair work on the steps leading from the sidewalk to the street. I had stopped to visit with a neighbor woman who had a small child with her.

When I turned to go back into my yard I saw a group of people, both men and women, standing around my front steps. Some of the women were in a wagon, like the kind the pioneers used to haul apples, potatoes and those kinds of things. All of them were dressed in white. I could see them as clearly as I have ever seen anything in my life. The white buttons on their clothing glistened in the morning sun. The men were wearing white shoes that looked brand new.

None of the people were moving or talking. They just looked at me and smiled. It was like they were a choir about ready to begin singing. Around the entire group, like a halo, was a warm, soft, gentle glow that extended upward and behind them as well.

"These are my people," I thought. I wondered why they had appeared to me. I had never seen anything like this in my entire life prior to this time, and never have since. I felt like I was filled with their love as they smiled at me. I had never seen anything so beautiful, so tender, so awesome. I don't know how long I just stood there and stared at them, filled with wonder and awe.

Eventually I looked down at my feet for an instant, and when I looked up they were gone.

I don't know why such a glorious manifestation was given to me. One of my neighbors thought they were people whose genealogy work I had recently completed. I don't know, only that I am very grateful to have seen the veil parted in such a glorious manner.

Chapter
Twelve

I Saw My Children
by Juliann Johnson Bradshaw

In 1982 Jeff and I had been married eight years, and we still had no children. I was pregnant for the third time, having gone through two miscarriages, and was anxiously awaiting the birth of our first child.

There were complications. The child was born premature at six months. It was a little girl. We named her Ruth Anne, after Ruth in the Bible. She died right after her birth.

I began praying with all my heart to know if there were any more children who were supposed to come to us. I didn't think I could handle another pregnancy that resulted in the loss of the embryo or child. I didn't feel like I could get pregnant again unless I had some kind of assurance that we would have a live child.

I believe it was the night after Ruth Anne's funeral that I woke up in the middle of the night to discover a young woman kneeling by the side of my bed. She had long, blond hair, and looked to be about 19 years old. She was dressed in white. There was a light radiating from her.

"Ruth Anne?" I asked.

"I am your daughter," she responded. "Come with me."

"Should I wake up your father?" I asked, looking over at Jeff who was still asleep.

"Not yet," she said. "We'll come back for him later."

The next thing I knew my spirit was rising above my body. I knew I was out of my body because I could look back down on the bed and see my body.

I was in the air floating towards the end of the room. The young woman was in front of me. When we reached the wall, it extended, and continued to extend as we moved along. Eventually we came to a stage. The young woman moved onto the stage after telling me to stay where I was. All communication took place mentally. There was no verbal exchange.

"Now you will meet your children," she said, turning to face me. She began to move about, almost like she was dancing. As I watched her, I began to feel what her spirit was like. She was very talented, and absolutely beautiful.

When she was finished she moved off the left side of the stage. The next thing I knew a boy was coming onto the stage from the right. He had dark hair and looked to be about 19 years old too. Instead of wearing white, he was dressed in ordinary street clothes—a plaid shirt and blue trousers. He didn't move around like the girl had done, but just stood there looking at me intently and smiling.

Eventually he moved off the left side of the stage just as the girl before him had done.

Another girl moved onto the stage from the right. She was younger than the first, maybe 12 or 13 years old. She had auburn hair. I thought to myself, "This is my Brittani." Brittani was a favorite name I was reserving for a daughter. She didn't move freely and gracefully like the other girl had done. This new little girl seemed to be encumbered or weighted down with something. She was wearing a blue outfit which seemed to be the cause of her sluggishness.

Finally she was able to shed the lower half of the blue outfit. Suddenly she was free to move and dance about like the first girl. She seemed very happy. When she finished she went the same way the other two had gone, off the left side of the stage.

No more children came onto the stage. I was told in my mind that it was time to go back to my bed. I wanted to see the blond girl again, but it was over. I went back down a long hall, eventually entering my bedroom where I re-entered my body.

I woke up Jeff and told him what had happened. He felt bad that he didn't get to share the experience with me.

Four months later we adopted a little girl with reddish-brown hair. We named her Brittani. Two years after that we had a little dark-haired son born to us.

There is no doubt in my mind that our son is the boy I saw on the stage. I think the second girl I saw, the one in the burdensome blue suit, was Brittani. The clothing that was weighing her down may be symbolic of her situation before we adopted her setting her free from her heavy burden.

I do know the first girl was Ruth Anne. Even though she did not respond to her name. It was only an earthly name given her after she died. She was never given a blessing. I believe when I called her Ruth, she was not used to being addressed by that name. I made a tiny white dress with lace and little pearls for her burial. She was wearing the same dress only a larger version when she visited me.

This experience was and has been of great comfort and guidance to me. I am so grateful to have been allowed to penetrate the veil to meet my children.

Chapter Thirteen

I Had to Go Back

by Fred Huston

I was born in Columbus, Ohio on October 9, 1919. There were 12 children in our family. At age four I came down with a severe case of diphtheria. The doctor would visit me at home. Today I would have probably been sent to a hospital.

One day I became worse and my mother sent for the doctor who examined me while my mother and father waited in the kitchen. When the doctor joined them he seemed very distressed.

"I am very sorry to tell you this," he said, "but we will have to start making burial plans. Your child is dead."

My parents later told me what the doctor had said. While all this was going on at home I was tumbling through space. There was nothing solid to hold onto. I was in what appeared to be a large tunnel, and there were bright lights.

Upon reaching the end of the tunnel I was able to stand up. I remember a person holding my right hand. He was dressed in white and surrounded by a beautiful aura, a soft golden light. We were in a place with beautiful buildings and golden pathways.

I saw a man sitting in a golden throne or chair. Two other people were walking down a path near him. They stopped to look at me.

"Take him back. He is not ready," said the man in the golden chair.

The next thing I remember, I was back in my body in the living room. My older sister, who was about ten at the time, was the first to notice my return. She hurried into the kitchen.

"You don't have to worry anymore," she told my mother and father. "I prayed for him and I asked God to send brother back."

Even though I was only four at the time, I have a vivid and clear memory of the events of that day. Over the years as I have thought about what happened I have concluded that I must have had some kind of mission to accomplish in life, or I wouldn't have been sent back.

That belief was reinforced in World War II when I was a gunner on a B-17 returning from a bombing mission over Germany. Our plane was hit and we went down in the North Sea. I was wounded and unconscious. All but the tail gunner were dead.

While the tail gunner was inflating the raft he checked some of the men around him for vital signs. Feeling I had a pulse he decided to put me in the raft. I weighed about 190 pounds at the time, and he couldn't have weighed much over a hundred. I don't know how he did it, only that it was some kind of miracle how he saved my life that night.

I later became a chemical engineer and worked for the water department for the city of Los Angeles. I have been a Baptist all my life, and am now retired and living in Utah. I am still not sure what mission my life was spared for on those two occasions.

Chapter Fourteen

Good Deeds Determined the Size of House

by Mary Hales

Late in the evening on May 9, 1925, four of us were heading south on Highway 89 south of Salt Lake City near Draper, Utah. My cousin, Lynn Hales, was driving the Franklin automobile. I had just finished my first year of teaching in Idaho and was anxious to

get home. It was Friday, and my fiance´, Vic
Frandsen, was in charge of the Gold and Green Ball
in Springville the next night. We were planning to be
married later that summer.

As we approached the Point of the Mountain, we
noticed that the headlights of an automobile
approaching from the south were swerving all over
the road. Almost before we realized what was
happening, the car cut across the road in front of us,
clear to the right edge of the pavement, then back into
the side of our car, and hit us right where I was
sitting on the right side.

We found out later the driver of the car that hit
us was drunk. He was a 37-year-old man on parole
from the state penitentiary. His companion was a 17-
year-old girl. Neither of them was seriously injured.

I was the only one in our vehicle with serious
injuries. I was taken to the county hospital in Salt
Lake City. Among numerous injuries I had a
crushed pelvis, my hip was ripped from the socket,
and my tongue was bitten off. Over the next five years
pieces of glass worked to the surface, coming out of
my ear, leg and other parts of my body.

I suppose I was lucky to be alive. My parents
were still mourning the loss of my older brother,
Howard, who had been killed in World War I.
Howard had graduated from Brigham Young
University where he played on the basketball team.
Everyone loved Howard. Many of his friends called
him Josh. He was the first man from Utah County to
enlist to fight in World War I. It devastated my

parents to learn he had been killed in action. After seven years they were still grieving the loss.

While I was not in critical condition, the doctors were very concerned about what to do with my crushed pelvis. A few days after the accident I remember a Dr. Baldwin coming in to see me. He said he hadn't slept all night, wondering what to do with my pelvis. He said I wouldn't be able to enjoy a normal married life, nor would I be able to have any children.

At that time the use of traction was still experimental, but he had been reading about it in medical journals and thought we ought to try it. They put me on a plank bed and began applying weights to my legs. The doctors had never done this before, so there was some experimentation as they manipulated my body, applying the different weights and pulleys. After two or three hours the pain became more than I could bear, finally forcing them to stop, at least temporarily.

The next thing I remember I was on top of a tall hill at the edge of a huge amphitheater filled with rows and rows of soldiers in uniform. They were listening to a speech by a man who was standing down in front of them.

I don't remember leaving my body, passing through a tunnel or anything like that. Like Paul said in the New Testament, I don't know if I was in or out of my body. All I know is that as clearly as I remember anything in my life, I was standing at the top of that amphitheater looking at all those soldiers.

I recognized the man speaking to them. It was my brother, Howard, who had been lost in action. He indicated that he recognized me too by smiling at me, but he continued his speech until he was finished.

After he delivered his sermon, he walked up to see me.

"What are you doing here?" he asked.

"I don't know," was my honest reply.

"It isn't your time yet," he said. We visited for a few minutes, then he said, "You haven't seen your little sister." He was referring to a sister who had been born several years before me, but had died of pneumonia when nine months old.

"Would you like to see her?" he asked. I said I would.

We started walking together through a place that was much like earth, but much more beautiful. It was a garden setting with many beautiful flowers of many colors and many green plants.

When we reached my sister, to my surprise, she still looked like a baby, but she seemed much more intelligent than a normal baby her size would be. She was with other children in a little clearing in a pine forest. The children were sitting on logs while women instructed them.

To my amazement I recognized the teachers. They were women I had known who had died. There was my mother's sister-in-law, Elenor Brockbank, who died at age 20, a Sister Prior who used to live in our neighborhood, one of Mother's cousins, and another sister-in-law named Zoe Brockbank.

The children were seated on sawed-off logs while the older women taught them. The children seemed happy, and the forest setting for their school was one of the most beautiful places I have ever seen.

"You might as well look around as long as you are here," my brother said, as we continued our walk through this beautiful place.

We saw many beautiful homes. He pointed out one as the one Joseph Smith lived in. I was surprised to see that while many of the homes were spacious, others were very small. Some were barely larger than a small kitchen, or large bathroom. I couldn't imagine why anyone would want to live in a house so small. I asked my brother about this.

"That was all the material they sent up," was his strange reply.

"What do you mean?" I asked.

"That was all the good works they sent up," he replied, meaning that the size of house one gets in paradise or heaven is determined by the quantity and quality of the good deeds performed.

I thought that was very interesting. Finally, Howard said, "Don't you think it's time you went back?"

It was after that that I heard the doctors telling my parents that they thought they could save my life, but that I would never walk again and wouldn't be able to have children.

Two or three weeks later my great uncle, Heber Jex, came in to see me. He asked if I wanted a blessing. I had already received a blessing from my father and brother, but didn't see where another could do any harm. I told him I would like that very much.

He laid his hands on my head and promised me that because of my faith, and the love I had for my Heavenly Father, I would walk without a limp.

Within an hour of the blessing a feeling like being stuck with pins came into my little toes. Within three days that feeling went all the way to my hips. I knew then I would walk again, and soon I was. I had a limp for about a year, but have never limped since that time.

The marriage with Vic was postponed. The doctor said we shouldn't marry for three years, so we waited. In the meantime I had to go through some very painful treatments to get my body as nearly back to normal as possible.

Before our marriage, the doctor said I should not attempt to have children, but if I insisted on trying, I should have them three years apart, and not have any more than three. And that's exactly what we did.

Our first child was a son. We named him Glen. Three years and three months later we had Lee, then three years and ten months later we had Ann. After that we had to stop.

While I was in the hospital after the accident, I told my parents about my experience with Howard, and how he had been preaching the gospel to all those soldiers. After that they felt much better about losing him, knowing he had a mission on the other side of the veil.

Chapter Fifteen

A Voice Told Him to Turn Off the Music

by Paula D. Smith

My husband, Mike, has had two experiences that reaffirm that there is indeed life after death. The first happened after we had been married for five years. We had gone through a long trying time of wanting to start a family, but not being able to do it.

Anyone who has gone through this knows how frustrating it can be.

I had reached a point where I wondered if God was even there, or if he loved me, and if he did why he wasn't allowing us to have children. During the lowest point of this period, Mike had an experience in the temple. We had gone there to pray and to receive some measure of peace concerning our inability to have children.

As Mike was changing into his temple clothes, he distinctly saw two people, a girl whom he thought was in her twenties, and a boy who looked a little younger. The boy was taller than the girl.

Mike said he did not see them like you and I see each other, but he saw them in his mind. He had the distinct impression they were the children who were waiting to come to us. They told him in his mind the time was very soon that they would come to join our family.

Later when Mike told me about this, I had the distinct and undeniable feeling that what he said was true. A month later I became pregnant with our first child, which was a little girl. Two and a half years after that we had another baby, a little boy.

I know these children were the two people my husband saw in the temple that night, and he was allowed to see them at a time when we desperately needed that confirmation.

The boy is seven months old at the time of this writing, and my husband has had the impression that we are going to have another girl. He says that from time to time he can feel her spirit lingering near, and that she is just waiting to join us also.

The second experience concerns my father who died ten years ago. Mike never met my father, and I often tell my husband I wish he had because my father was such a good man.

One weekend we went to my mother's home to visit. She needed some help around the yard. I had told Mike that Mother could use his help all day just to do things around the outside of the house.

When we arrived Mother told Mike she needed a new door on a shed out back. That was an area of the yard where my father used to spend a lot of time building things, working on old cars, and just tinkering.

Mike went out to work on the door. He was wearing his walkman so he could listen to music as he worked. He hadn't been there long when he thought he heard a voice telling him to turn off the music and listen. There being no one else around, he ignored the prompting. But then he heard the same thing two more times.

Finally, Mike turned off the Walkman and listened. Suddenly the warmest feeling of peace and love came over him, so strong that he had to sit down. He knew my father was there. He could see him in his mind and hear my father talking to him, so he just sat there, enveloped in this wonderful feeling.

My father told Mike he was glad to have him as a son-in-law, and that he loved me, his daughter, very much. My father said he was waiting for my mother to join him. He said he had a special message for her about my little brother who is an alcoholic with many problems. He told Mike to tell Mother to let her worries about my brother rest, that the boy had his own life to live. He told Mike again how much he loved him and me and how glad he was Mike was in the family.

About this time I looked outside and noticed something not quite right about the way Mike was just sitting there, so I went out to him.

"Your father is here right now," he said, when I looked at him. Again I knew, like that time in the temple, that what Mike was telling me was true. I felt the same warm feeling, knowing that my father was there and that he loved us. We sat there crying together, basking in the wonderful feeling of peace and love. It was as if my father had his arm around us and all cares and worries were far away.

I know without doubt that we lived before we came to earth, and we will live after we leave this earth. These two wonderful experiences help affirm this. I witness and testify that this is true.

Chapter Sixteen

The Light Entered My Body

by Molly Roderick

My first near-death experience occurred in 1959 at the birth of my second child, Carl, in International Falls, Minnesota. I remember being in labor a long time, and pushing so hard. But the baby went up instead of down. The afterbirth came out first, and I began to bleed badly.

They tied something around my upper abdomen to force the baby down, but it didn't seem to work. The bleeding worsened. They didn't have my blood type, so one of the nurses had to find a lady on the street who was willing to give me some blood.

Suddenly I found myself in the air above my body, looking down. I could see the doctors and nurses, and could hear them talking. Then I was in a dark tunnel moving towards a bright light, but before I reached the light I was back in the hospital room looking down at my body again. Then I was back in my body as they pulled the baby out.

I had a similar experience in 1973 while in a Portland hospital for open heart surgery. The operation had already taken place and I was in the recovery room, when something went wrong. I was losing blood. Suddenly I was in the dark, swirling through a dark tunnel again, towards the same bright light.

The next thing I knew I was back in the operating room, above my body, looking down. I could see everything including the doctors and nurses. I could hear them talk, but they were not aware of my being there, above them in the air. The valves were having trouble seeding as the doctors called it. They thought they would have to open me up again, but didn't. They were giving me alot of blood.

Then I was back in my body again. When I recovered, I didn't tell anyone what had happened. I was sure they would think I was nuts.

My most memorable near-death experience was July, 1989. We had just returned home from the dedication of the new LDS temple in Portland. At that time, after two open heart operations, my heart was still giving me trouble, making it necessary for me to attend the dedication in a wheel chair. I'll never forget entering the Celestial Room. I felt the spirit of the Lord so strong that I couldn't hold back the tears. Those who know me know that I do not cry easily, but I did in the temple that day. Never had I felt the spirit so strong.

Upon retiring to bed that night, I couldn't sleep. I felt terrible, and the pains in my chest continued to worsen.

Finally, about two a.m., we called the 911 number for help. When the paramedics arrived they hooked me up to the EKG monitor. They said that while the reading was somewhat erratic, they didn't think anything was seriously wrong with me, that I ought to go back to bed.

I knew better. Something was very wrong. As soon as they left, my husband, Maurice rushed me to the hospital in our car.

Immediately they hooked me up to various machines and began making tests. They determined from an angiogram the next morning that my heart arteries had a 98% blockage. My condition was so serious that one doctor said there was only a ten percent chance of me ever leaving the hospital alive.

As they began making preparations for surgery I had a heart attack. Maurice had already called for the children and some of them had arrived. As I went into surgery I was telling them how much I loved them, and saying goodbye to them.

I didn't think I was going to make it this time. I had been praying every spare moment that I would be able to see my grandchildren again, and my son, Maurice Jr., who had not yet arrived. I was a nervous wreck. I was very frightened.

I wasn't ready to die. I didn't think I was worthy to make it to heaven, or the Celestial Kingdom. I was not ready to meet or face my Heavenly Father. I had started going to church about six months earlier in a sincere effort to get my life in order.

It was so hard to say goodbye to my husband. There were so many things I wanted to tell him, and I know there were things he wanted to tell me. Through all the years of struggling we still had each other. He was my best friend, my lover, my counselor and sounding board, and my partner. He's the only one I can trust with all the feelings of my heart, and he understands. There could never be another man for me. After 32 years of marriage our love was still growing.

They gave me a shot and the next thing I remember, the operation was over and I was in intensive care. The operation had started about noon, and it was now about 8 p.m. that night.

Dr. Baldwin, the man who operated on me, came into my room. He patted my leg and began talking to me.

"Molly, wake up, now. Can you hear me?"

I tried to say yes, but there was a big tube in my throat. I was finally able to grunt.

"That's a good girl," he said. "You did real well. You were quite a trooper in there."

There was a pause, silence. I could hear one of the machines start to beep.

"Oh, dear God," Dr. Baldwin said. Then I could hear him calling to someone to get the defibulators. After shocking me three times with those awful things, I could hear him telling someone they would have to open me up. I started praying to my Heavenly Father.

What happened next is still hard for me to talk about, but it happened and I can remember it clearly.

It was as if a bright light descended from above and entered my being. It became brighter and brighter until it seemed like it might consume me. I heard a voice.

"Molly, you are a good person," said a soft, beautiful, male voice. I'm sure it was the voice of my Heavenly Father. I didn't see a face, and I don't recall my spirit leaving my body. There was only the bright light, and the voice, which continued to speak to me, in response to my thoughts. I would think about something that had been troubling me, and the voice would respond.

"You can do anything you choose to do. Your time is not up yet. There are things for you to do on the earth."

"All of your children will be active members in the church, and the men will hold the priesthood."

The light continued to get brighter until it totally consumed me.

"You can be a queen, Molly. You can go higher and higher. There is no end to the glory you can have if you just keep my commandments. You and your husband will go together."

I had always worried about dying and leaving Maurice behind.

The voice said some things about my children and their spouses, and my grandchildren. My Lord spoke to me a long time. He answered many questions, and told me many things in addition to answering my questions. He removed all the doubts I had had about the truthfulness of the gospel.

Earlier, I had had a serious addiction to smoking, which was undoubtedly the major cause of my heart problems, but no matter how hard I tried it seemed I just couldn't get rid of those awful cigarettes. The voice told me I would no longer have a problem with that. Since that night in the hospital ten months have passed, and I can honestly say I have not craved a cigarette, not once.

I have talked to Doctor Baldwin since the operation. He said they opened me up a second time right there in the I.C.U. He massaged my heart for twenty minutes, then he followed the stretcher down the hall where he worked on me for another four hours. He had to take my heart out and put it in a pan of saline solution while I was hooked up to the heart-lung machine. He said my heart stopped a second time and he worked with it another fifteen minutes to get it going. He said by all medical standards I should have been dead. He said he didn't know why he kept working on me because they usually give up on a heart after about ten minutes.

Three months after the operation, October 14, 1989, Maurice and I were sealed in the temple.

I don't know why the Lord chose me to talk to after my surgery. All I know is that it happened, and it changed my life. And I hope that by allowing this to be published others may perhaps benefit from what happened to me.

Chapter
Seventeen

I Had No Power to Communicate

by Charles John Lambert

As published in the Juvenile Instructor, page 359, 1886.

When I was about thirteen years old I was on the point of leaving my home to go to the vicinity of the Jordan River (Salt Lake Valley) to bring the family cow from the pasture. As I was departing my mother said, "Charles John, you must not go into the water."

I fully intended to comply with this wish, but when I reached the pasture I set aside my scruples regarding disobedience to my parent and, in company with Harrison Shurtliff, entered a tributary of the Jordan, near where it emptied into the stream, to bathe.

We amused ourselves tumbling over a log that lay in the water. In going down I caught under this log, was there held fast, and found it impossible to reach the surface. I knew I was drowning, and as the water gurgled down my throat a sleepy, painless sensation pervaded me, then all was blank.

When I recovered consciousness I was no longer in the body, but my spirit was out of the water.

No human power could describe my condition. Every action, and even every thought of my life—good, bad and indifferent—was clearly before my comprehension. I could not tell by what process this effect was produced, but I knew that my whole life in detail was before my view with terrible clearness.

One idea seemed more vivid than the rest—the fact that I had lost my life by my own sinful act—disobedience to my mother.

There were spiritual persons with me, and I understood that they also knew all about the nature of the deeds I had done in the body. They appeared to have taken charge of me in the spirit, and I seemed to be on the most familiar terms with them.

I saw Harrison Shurtliff looking for my body in great excitement, but I had no power to communicate with him. I looked into the water and beheld my body, and wondered why he did not see it. Then I observed that I saw clear through the log, under which the body was lying.

I saw young Shurtliff, after looking for it in vain, run along the bank a distance of about two blocks, and tell John Harker what had taken place. The two then came rapidly to the spot where the drowning occurred.

I discovered that I could move about without the slightest effort and with great rapidity.

My spirit friends took me away from the scene of the incident and in a twinkling, as it were, I was in the city. They told me that my death was caused by disobedience to my parent. I felt keenly on this point, and informed them that if I were allowed to re-enter my body I should never be guilty of the same sin again. I was then informed that I might return to it.

In an instant—almost as quick as thought—I was at the spot where the drowning occurred and saw my body lying on the bank. Young Shurtliff and John Harker had placed it in such a position that the head was downhill and they were working hard to get the water to flow from the mouth. It looked loathsome to me, notwithstanding I had expressed a desire to return to it.

Suddenly I became insensible to what transpired. I began to recover sensibility in my body, to which I had returned in the interval that appeared blank. My agony while recovering was fearful. It seemed as if the suffering of an ordinary lifetime had been concentrated into a few minutes' duration. It appeared as if every sinew of my physical system was being violently torn out.

This gradually subsided. I was raised to my feet. Some boys took charge of my cow, and others helped me to go to the city.

On arriving in town I had so far recovered as to be able to walk alone, and wended my way home. I was so thoroughly ashamed of my conduct that I carefully concealed what had happened from the knowledge of my mother. She did not learn of it for several weeks, and would not have learned of it then had not John Harker visited the house.

On seeing me he remarked, "Is this not the boy who was drowned while down at the pasture after the cow?" Then turning to me he said, "You are the boy, are you not?"

I was in the act of slinking out of the house when this question was put, but I, of course, answered that I was the boy in question. This was news to mother, who felt quite excited about it.

The incident narrated above made an indelible impression upon my mind, and doubtless has more or less influenced my life since it occurred. Some people may think that the statements regarding my leaving the body are based upon imagination. What I have described, however, was as real as anything could be, and was not imaginary. While my spirit was separate from its earthly (counterpart) I saw and understood all that took place, as was afterwards verified by the parties whom I have named in connection with the drowning.

The effect produced upon me has been to cause me to avoid ever disobeying my parents. I have never, from that time to the present, so far as I know, acted contrary to their expressed wishes, and I trust I never shall. I have therefore kept the condition upon which I appeared to be allowed to again take possession of my body.

Thus ends the story of my experience in being drowned and coming to life again. The incident may serve to point a moral by which some young people may profit.

Chapter Eighteen

She Was Wearing a Sun Dress

by Eleanor M. Sinden

In 1961 my stepson, my husband's son by a previous marriage, was driving his new convertible from Lake Tahoe to Reno. In attempting to pass a car, another vehicle pulled out in front of both cars, causing a collision. Rex's car was forced over the embankment, rolling 350 feet down a steep gully.

He, of course, sustained many injuries and was rushed to the hospital in Reno. Some object had passed clear through his neck so fast the doctors could not tell if it was metal or wood.

Rex and I rushed to Reno, and checked into a motel near the hospital. Rex Jr. was alive, but in a coma.

The sixth evening after the accident, I was in the motel bathroom, when I suddenly looked up and saw Rex Jr. He was in his hospital nightgown, stretched out on the same thermal mattress the hospital was using to keep his temperature down. He was looking at me with his usual beautiful, happy face. He didn't say a word. He just looked at me and smiled, as if everything was all right.

I rushed into the bedroom to tell Rex I had seen his son, and that the boy was happy.

"What is he trying to tell us?" I asked.

"That everything is going to be all right," Rex answered, calmly. He had been stretched out on the bed reading the Bible.

"Does this mean he is going to live?"

"I don't know," Rex said. "Whether he lives or dies, he just wants us to know that everything is all right, and that we shouldn't worry about him."

The next day Rex Jr. died.

Five years later, 1966, my sister-in-law passed away. At the time of her death, she was a member of the Christian Science Church, but was very restless in her religious beliefs. She was not satisfied, and was looking for something more.

A few weeks after her death, I woke up in the middle of the night. I was facing Rex, and had the distinct impression that I should turn over. I did so. My sister-in-law was standing by the bed looking at me. She was wearing a sun dress, one that came off the shoulder with no sleeves. I had seen her wear it many times. She just stood there and looked at me. There was no conversation. Whereas in life she had been a cheerful and happy woman, she now appeared troubled and worried.

I belonged to the Presbyterian Church at the time, and when I told the minister what had happened he said I was batty, that things like that just didn't happen.

During the next few months I saw my sister-in-law two more times. Both times she was wearing the same dress. Both times she had the same troubled expression.

It was during this time that her husband joined the LDS church. As soon as it was possible he had her baptized by proxy and sealed to him. After that happened, she never appeared to me again. I strongly suspect she finally found the peace she had been looking for.

Chapter Nineteen

She Shall Live

by Alvin Day
for the Improvement Era, January, 1947
Provided by Art Day of Provo, UT

It was a beautiful summer day in the little settlement of Mount Pleasant, Utah. The year was 1862, and the little group of pioneers had been there but three short years. Already the place had been greatly changed. The sagebrush and the sandstone boulders had been cleared away, and many log homes had been built.

Fast growing poplar trees were beginning to bring some shade to the walks along the broad well-laid-out streets. Every home had its vegetable garden, and many had young apple orchards. It had taken hard toil to subdue this little semi-desert part of the earth with a very limited number of implements and tools these pioneers had been able to bring across the plains with them or had obtained later.

Just one and a half blocks north of the partly built fort, which had taken so much hard labor to build, lived Nathan Staker and his wife, Eliza. Before two Mormon missionaries had found him, Staker had been a Methodist minister, but he recognized the voice of the restored gospel and obeyed it. He had come as a widower with a large family from Ontario, Canada.

Eliza Staker, who had been Eliza Burton, had heard and accepted the gospel with her husband, Joseph Burton, in Yorkshire, England, and promised him on his deathbed that she would bring their two young children to Zion. In spite of all the opposition of her prosperous English family, she had kept that promise. In addition to a hard sea voyage, she and her children suffered the trials of the Martin handcart company.

Nathan and Eliza had met at Pleasant Grove, Utah, and married in 1857. In the spring of 1859, they moved with the original settlers to build their humble home in Mount Pleasant.

On this summer day in 1862, Nathan had been working with his young apple trees. He had planted an acre of them, many fine varieties that were to be a delight to his children and his grandchildren. Four-year-old James liked to help his father in the garden and orchard, but his mother objected to his playing in the orchard because of the irrigation ditch which ran through it just beyond the garden gate. He had come in wet more than once from falling into it. Eliza kept a close watch to see that this garden gate was always fastened because of her toddling little Eliza Jane, who was only eighteen months old and who also liked to follow her father.

After his noonday meal and chores, Nathan went back to his work in the orchard. He did not notice that little Eliza Jane had followed him. Perhaps she was just a minute or two behind him.

Eliza soon missed her baby and began to look for her. The little girl was not around the house or garden, so Eliza called to her husband. The baby was not with him, and he hadn't seen her; it was very unusual for her to be lost, so he went to help look for her. They made a search of their premises but didn't find her. They went to the neighbor's, and soon the whole neighborhood joined in the search without success.

Then someone thought of the irrigation ditch.

Brother Staker hurried through the garden gate to the little footbridge and followed the ditch down to the lower end of the orchard. There, floating in the water, and lodged against the dam which Henry Wilcox had made to divert the water to his garden, he found the motionless body of his baby girl. He lifted her quickly out of the water and hurried to the house. Nathan, his wife, and the neighbors used every method known to them to revive little Eliza Jane, but failed.

During the excitement some of the group had seen a white-topped buggy go by. There was only one carriage like that in the county, and everyone knew it belonged to Apostle Orson Hyde, commonly known as Elder Hyde, who lived in Spring City, five miles to the south.

At Nathan's request, a neighbor went on horseback to overtake Elder Hyde and ask him to return and administer to the child. On his return, the apostle walked slowly through the garden to the little two-room log home and past tear-stained faces to where he was shown the body of little Eliza. Nathan asked him if he would administer to his little girl and call her back to life.

Orson Hyde examined the little body in silence. He could detect no pulse, and no beat of the tiny heart. The body was getting cold.

"How long was the little girl in the water?" he asked.

Brother Staker examined his watch.

"It's just about an hour since I went to the orchard, and I suppose she followed me," he said.

"I am very sorry, Brother and Sister Staker," the apostle said, "but I have examined your baby thoroughly, and she is dead, and it isn't pleasing in the sight of the Lord that we should try to bring back our dead after he has called them home."

Nathan was quite disturbed by the statement, and answered, "Elder Hyde, I have always tried to bow to the will of the Lord in all things, and am willing to now, but one thing troubles me very much. Soon after our little girl was born, a year and a half ago, we took her to Bishop Seeley to give her a blessing and a name. I gave her that blessing myself, and I distinctly remember that I promised her that she should grow to womanhood and become a mother in Israel. I sincerely believe that such promises made by the authority of the priesthood will be fulfilled, but now..." he broke off and gestured helplessly.

"In that case," Elder Hyde answered, "I will ask God to restore your little girl to life again, and if that promise was made in the spirit of faith and righteousness, she shall live again to fulfil it."

The exact words that Orson Hyde uttered in his administration to little Eliza Staker at that time are not recorded or remembered, but he called her back to life, and she came. The next day she was playing with her little homemade toys again, toys which by comparison with those of today would seem crude, but which were very dear to her.

She did live to womanhood, and became a mother. She married Eli A. Day, a young school teacher who had been chosen in those days of community planning to go to the University of Deseret and study, to introduce new methods of teaching to the Mount Pleasant school. To them were born thirteen children. The promise made by her father at the time of her infant blessing was fulfilled.

Chapter Twenty

I Exploded from My Body

by Richard Nelson

On July 6, 1948 Alice Becker entered the Madison General Hospital in Madison, Wisconsin to give birth to her second child. She was 24 years old, had a wonderful husband, and a sweet little girl. Her life was comfortable and happy, and she was elated to be bringing another child into her precious family circle.

Childbirth is never simple, though. The possibility of life threatening complications is always present. It is ironic that a woman must pass so close to death to bring life into the world. In Alice's situation she not only passed close to death, but she met him face to face and journeyed with him for a while.

At first it appeared that the delivery would be just another routine operation, everything was going perfectly. That is until it was time for the baby to leave the womb. Normally, the baby comes out followed by the placenta, but in this situation the placenta came out first causing massive hemorrhaging.

When this particular complication arises the doctors have a choice of either saving the mother or the child, rarely do both make it through alive. But this time it was different. Thanks to the skillful work of the physicians, both Alice and her baby, Barbara, lived through the ordeal.

Death, having been foiled once, decided to give Alice another try. No one is exactly sure what happened next, but after the ordeal was over the doctors working on Alice decided that there was probably some water that got into her I.V. without anyone noticing. Blood began to trickle out of her ear before anyone realized something was wrong. Inside, Alice felt like she was going to explode at any moment. It kept getting worse and worse until finally the anguish was so tremendous she decided she had had enough and could take no more. At this point she silently screamed, "Oh God! Take me!"

Instantly she felt an explosion which threw her clear of all the fear, pain, and anguish she had been fighting with only moments before. She had no idea what had happened, she only knew that she felt more peaceful and content than she had ever felt before. As she began to take notice of her surroundings she realized she was completely immersed in a flood of heavenly light. It seemed to her that the peace and contentment she was feeling was radiating directly from the light itself. It was almost as if the light was God.

Later in her life as she pondered over this experience she realized that unlike other people who had had similar experiences and found themselves in a long dark tunnel with a light at the end, Alice found herself entirely surrounded by the bright light without walking through a tunnel. Her explanation for this difference in experience was that she had actually called out for God to come and get her and he did.

While she was standing in the light trying to figure out where she was, she noticed she was slowly moving upwards, like she was in a slow elevator. She turned her head to look around and, below her, she saw a number of men dressed in surgical garb huddling around a young woman lying on a gurney, her long dark hair hanging off the edge of the table. Alice remembered thinking to herself that the woman was pretty, and casually wondered what was wrong with her. Then it finally hit her that she was looking at herself; she had somehow become detached and was looking down at her dead body.

She felt no remorse or longing to return to her body. To her she felt perfectly normal, almost like she still had her body. She had felt it when she turned her head and could feel the sensation of going up, as if she were in her usual physical condition. She had escaped from her pain and she felt great.

Suddenly she realized she was faced with a decision she would consciously have to make. She had two choices, she could either return to her body and continue on with her happy life and have the opportunity to raise her two daughters, or she could stay where she was, in the world of spirits. As she thought about all the good things that awaited her if she returned, mainly her husband and small family, she could not ignore the way she was feeling as she basked in the emotional warmth of the light. She decided she was more content where she was and made the decision to stay.

Off in the distance she noticed some rooms, the details of which she does not clearly remember, but she did know, somehow, that her grandfather was in one of them. It was as though they had never been apart. It was nice to know he was there, but she had more important things to think about.

When she made the decision to stay, the "elevator" began to pick up speed, rocketing upward, carrying her toward some unknown yet pleasant destination. As Alice was speeding along she began to think of all the promises she had made to people which would not be kept if she died; she began to worry. She spoke to the light as if it were God himself and said, "God, I can't go now, I've made promises. I've got to go back and keep them."

Immediately she found herself back in her body. She noticed that getting back into her body was much easier and more pleasant than it had been to exit it.

As soon as she realized she was back, she heard the nurse say, "Doctor, she's with us again!" Alice was allowed to keep her promises.

Alice told me this story in the fall of 1989 in Reno, Nevada. I was a missionary, teaching Alice about the Church of Jesus Christ of Latter-day Saints. As my companion and I taught her about the spirit world she began telling us what it was like to be there. She also told us a number of other experiences she had had dealing with those in the world of spirits. Soon we began to see how spiritually gifted Alice was. There were many times when we would sit for hours listening to experience after experience, marvelling at how in tune she was to the other side. She was baptized a few weeks later, and is now happily looking forward to the time when she can return to the sublime peace she felt during her visit beyond the veil.

Chapter Twenty-one

She Already Had a Calling

by Sharon McQueen
as told to Richard Nelson

I first met Mara in 1986 when she and her husband, with their young family, moved into our neighborhood in Orem, Utah. Our daughters, who had become friends, introduced us and we became immediate bosom buddies. Mara was half Japanese and very beautiful. She always wore a dress and was very conscious of her appearance; she always looked her best no matter what she was doing.

We began spending a lot of time together, often staying up all night at one of our houses, just talking, like school girls. We knew everything about each other, even some things our husbands didn't know. This closeness proved to be a tremendous blessing.

Almost a year to the day from when I met Mara, an event happened which drastically changed both our lives. I had just returned home from getting ice cream cones with the kids when my husband told me the police had called and asked for me. With apprehension I called to see what they had wanted and was startled at the news.

They told me that Mara had passed out while she was driving her car, and crashed. They had tried getting in touch with her husband to let him know what happened, but he was out of town, so one of the girls who was home gave them my phone number and told them I was her closest friend.

As soon as I got the news I rushed to the hospital to visit her. When I got there Mara was lying in her hospital bed in a semi-conscious state of mind. Also in the room were some of her extended family who had been contacted. One of the effects the accident had on Mara was to give her a temporary case of amnesia. She couldn't remember her husband, her children, or the people who were in the room when I got there, but when I went up to her she looked at me and said, "Sharon." I was the only one she recognized.

After numerous tests, CAT scans, and finally a radio scan, the doctors located a tumor the size of a nickel behind the optic nerve in Mara's brain. They said it had probably been there all her life and that it was benign.

The tumor had grown from its initial size to the size of a lemon. She had an operation to get it removed which was unsuccessful, yet the doctors still insisted it was not malignant and that she would be all right.

I didn't believe them for a second and decided to find out for myself how Mara was going to fare. That night, with all my heart I prayed to find out if Mara was going to live. After I was asleep I had a vivid dream of Mara's funeral. Later on I realized I had seen her funeral exactly as it would happen, down to the very finest of details. My prayer had been answered, and I knew she was going to die.

Mara's health went downhill fast as the tumor continued to grow, and we all knew her time to leave mortality was drawing near. During the next few months I spent a lot of time with her, just talking. She was petrified of dying, even though she understood the plan of salvation. She needed as much support as we could give her.

One morning when I went in to see her, she told me about an experience she had had the night before. She said she woke up from her sleep and found herself floating about ten feet above her body, looking down. She knew she was dead and pleaded to Heavenly Father not to take her because she felt her children were not prepared yet. She wanted some more time to get them ready for the inevitable. She was allowed to come back. This experience helped disperse some of the fear she had about dying, but not all of it.

The last time I saw her alive was July 3rd, almost a year after the tumor was first discovered. She had gone blind, had a stroke that crippled the right side of her body, and had wasted away to virtually nothing. We knew it would be a bitter-sweet blessing when she died. She hung on through the 4th and died on the morning of the 5th, a fast Sunday.

Before she died she asked me to attend her funeral, which was going to be held in the state of Washington, where her home was. So, the next morning I was vacuuming my car, getting ready for the trip; I was taking Mara's husband and kids with me. As I was vacuuming with our noisy shop-vac, I heard a voice, clearer than any I have ever heard, ask me,

"Why are you cleaning the car when my kids will only mess it up?" It was Mara's voice.

"I always clean my car when I go on a trip," I answered.

"You can hear me!" she exclaimed.

I think she was more surprised that I heard her, than I was that she was talking to me. She told me she had been trying to talk to her husband but he couldn't hear her. She had me call him and tell him to go downstairs so she could talk to him, which he did. I then felt her presence leave.

Two hours later I was fixing lunch for my husband who was home on a lunch break, when I felt Mara's presence enter the room. What followed was our longest and most interesting conversation. Although my husband couldn't hear her, he still participated in the discussion as I spoke the words. I was hearing Mara on a different level of communication, possibly through my thoughts. She, on the other hand, only heard me when I spoke out loud, she could not read my thoughts.

I asked her where she was and she responded, "I'm up." When she said that, I knew she meant between 18 and 24 inches above the ground. I asked her how she got around and she said she just moved. She didn't walk or fly or anything we could imagine, she just moved.

My next question was, "What is it like there?" In answer to this she began talking and talking, describing in every detail the new world she was in.

She said there were two levels; the one she was on, above the ground, and the one on the ground level with us. The spirits on the ground level wander aimlessly, not knowing where to go or what to do until they accept the gospel, at which point they move to the upper level. The people on the upper level could see us mortals as well as the spirits on the lower level of their world. But, the spirits on the lower level could only see their level.

She described to us how all the men on her level were teaching those on the level below. Everyone had a job to do and kept very busy, even she had already been given a calling, though she didn't mention to me what it was. She also said that everyone speaks the same language where she was.

Mara then began telling us how you know everyone when you get there. She said she had met all the latter-day prophets, from Joseph Smith down to Spencer W. Kimball who had just died. Then she made a statement that really made me realize what sort of atmosphere Mara was actually in.

Softly she said, "Sharon, Jesus' eyes really are blue." Then she went on to describe what it was like to be around Him and feel His love.

She said that where she was there were thousands upon thousands of bookshelves stuffed with books. There were books on every topic imaginable. But you didn't read them, all you had to do was open up a book and you would immediately absorb all the knowledge it contained. You could just sit down and learn anything you ever wanted to know. To learn everything would take an incredibly long time, though, because there were so many of them.

When we asked her if the people there wore white clothing, she responded that you could if you wanted to, but you didn't have to.

"I'm wearing peach," she said. This became an important statement because a day or so later Mara appeared to one of her daughters. When I asked the girl what she was wearing she said she had on a peach-colored dress—I had not mentioned to her that Mara told me what she was wearing.

Mara then told me there was a boy up there waiting to come down and join my family. I had not had any children for eight years and wasn't expecting any more, but sure enough, about a year later I gave birth to my third child, a precious little boy.

She said there were other babies too, from time to time, but they didn't stay long.

I asked her if she was going to her viewing, and to my surprise she said no. When I asked her why, she said that she didn't want to see a bunch of people crying over her shell (body).

"That's not me," she said. "I don't even look like that." That sounded like a good enough reason to me.

Sometimes during our conversation I couldn't understand her because she was talking faster than I could think. I had to ask her a number of times to slow down so I could hear what she was saying. Although she was talking rapidly, it seemed like she was talking to me as slow as she possibly could. I know I missed a lot of what she was telling me because of this.

We talked for about an hour, enjoying each other's company once more. Finally, she had to leave to visit her husband again and I felt her presence leave.

Mara talked to me two more times during the next couple of days; she became more and more difficult to understand each time. The first of these visits occurred while we were driving up to Washington. She spoke to both her husband and me at the same time. Her last visit was at the funeral and only lasted for a few minutes.

The reason she came back was to comfort those of us who desperately needed to know she was fine and that everything was going to be all right. Now, because of this experience, I no longer fear death. I consider this to be a great spiritual blessing, for now I know a little more of what to expect when I die. I remember vividly how happy and serene Mara seemed during our visits, and I know that I will experience the same thing when it is my turn to pass beyond the veil.

Chapter
Twenty-two
A Straight-liner
by Annette Long

In the summer of 1989, my doctor detected a cyst near my ovary and decided it should be removed. He assured me this was a fairly routine operation, that I probably wouldn't even be in the hospital overnight.

I felt differently, and I don't know why. I began to get my affairs in order in the event I didn't make it. My loved ones tried to tell me I was overreacting. But I somehow seemed to know that I was approaching a major turning point in my life and perhaps wouldn't be around to tell about it. I had never felt that way before.

The operation took place at Mountain View Hospital in Payson, Utah, August 16, 1989. I made it through the surgery all right, even though the doctors had to remove more than just the cyst. By the time they were through I had had a total hysterectomy.

The next thing I remember was waking up in the recovery room, feeling awful—like I might die. I told the nurse that I felt really sick, that she had to help me. I found out later I was having some adverse reaction to the medication I had received. When additional medication was prescribed the reaction only worsened, and all my vital signs stopped, including my heart beat.

What happened next was not a dream. Dreams are vague and fleeting. What I experienced was real. I was in a room, but not a hospital room, lying on my back, surrounded by people in white clothing—not fancy and bright, but more casual and subdued in style and brightness. One lady with silver hair had it tied in a bun.

These strange people were standing around me, asking me what I wanted to do. I would guess their number to be about fifteen. Several were touching me where I had been operated on. Two were standing by my head, holding my hands. I didn't recognize any of them, but I could feel their love and concern for me, especially the two who were holding my hands. I had never felt such comfort, such love. I didn't know who they were at the time, but I was sure I had known them before. I have since concluded they were my heavenly father and Jesus.

"I want a blessing, and I want to go home," I responded. I had been concerned about not receiving a blessing before I entered the hospital. Several of them put their hands on my head and gave me the blessing. I cannot remember what they said.

Though I could feel the comfort and love from the people around me, I was nervous and upset about what was happening. I could hardly believe this was happening to me.

I realized I had a choice. I could stay with these wonderful people, or I could return. I understood I would face difficulties if I chose to return. I also understood there was a mission for me to fill, or something special for me to do if I returned, so that is what I chose to do. Besides, I had four children that needed a mother.

I don't remember returning to my body, only waking up in the hospital room, marveling about what had happened. I learned later I had been in intensive care for some time, my life apparently in the balance. But I can't remember any of that.

When the doctors came in to see me, they talked about death, and assured me I should not worry about what had happened. At first I wondered how they knew because I had told them nothing. They said I had died, calling me a straight-liner, a reference to when the graph line levels out on the heart machine, indicating the heart has stopped beating.

In the coming months I felt a lot of frustration, still not knowing what the mission was I had returned to do. I thought about that a lot, but could come up with no answers. My patriarchal blessing told me that following a struggle with my health I would become a great leader. I'm still not sure how a working woman with four children can be a great leader.

I do know, however, that my fear of death is gone. Before this experience I always had faith in a life after death, but now I know there is life after death, and that there are people on the other side who watch over and love me, and are concerned about my welfare. It will be a glorious reunion when I return to them. I hope the next time I will know who they are.

In the meantime I am anxiously waiting to find out about that very special mission I was allowed to come back to accomplish.

Chapter Twenty-three

He Pushed Me Back Into My Body

by Marc Shelton

When I was a year old a tumor started growing on the left side of my face. It grew bigger and bigger until it was as large as a grapefruit, totally disfiguring my face. The doctors said I had neurofibromatosis, or elephant man's disease.

As I grew older I lost a leg to the disease, and by the time I was 22 the tumor was getting so large that it was just a matter of time until it would cut off my breathing. I was desperate. I knew I would die if the tumor was not removed.

Then I was examined by Dr. Bruce Leipzig at the University of Arkansas hospital in Little Rock. He said he thought the tumor might be isolated and hadn't grown through and around other tissue as most other doctors seemed to think. He was willing to do his best to remove it.

The surgery was scheduled and I was admitted to the hospital and the operation was performed.

The doctors said the operation was a success. The next day I felt good enough to want to go home. The doctors were surprised I felt so good. I had used 15 pints of blood during the operation.

On the third day when Dr. Leipzig came in to see me I began to take a turn for the worse. He detected abnormal swelling in my face. He discovered blood clots and decided emergency surgery was needed.

I remember just before the operation, kneeling on my hospital bed, pleading with the Lord to spare my life, promising that if I lived through the operation I would serve him the remainder of my life. After a brief diversion as a teenager into drugs and alcohol, I was making a valiant effort to get my life in order, and had just recently received my LDS temple endowments preparatory to going on a mission.

After my prayer they wheeled me into the operating room. The doctors and aids strapped me to the operating table, flat on my back my arms extended straight out. One of my thoughts was how funny that an operating table is shaped much like a cross. I couldn't move, not even my head.

After applying some local anesthetic they began inserting various life support tubes prior to putting me under. The doctor who was numbing my throat with a cotton swab, continued to apologize for the discomfort he was causing me. A laryngoscope was pushed down my throat to keep the passageway open and clear for a tube which went into my lungs. The general anesthetic couldn't be applied until all the life support tubes were in place.

While all this was happening I suddenly passed out.

The next thing I remember was being able to sit up. This was both surprising and confusing to me because I remembered how tightly the doctors had strapped me down. Yet, I was sitting up, easily and comfortably. In fact, all the pain and discomfort were suddenly gone. I had a feeling of overwhelming peace. The trauma and stress were gone. It was like I was standing beside a clear blue lake under an apple tree on a beautiful summer day, a cool breeze blowing in my face.

I could see the doctors, standing around me, doing their various jobs. But I could see other people too. They were dressed in white robes. The material the robes were made from was not like silk or satin, but more substantial, like tweed or homespun.

I was filled with a feeling of total peace. All the fear I had felt earlier was gone. For the first time in years my body was totally free of pain. I realized I was dying, and I was happy. I had no desire to go back.

I was in transition between the physical world and the spirit world. I was halfway between two plains of existence, and could see both. There was a kind of a greenish hue to the physical world where the doctors worked on me. The spirit world was more subdued in color, not bright at all.

I don't know how much time was passing while all this was taking place. It seemed to me like a long time, but in the physical world it may have only been a few seconds. I don't know.

Eventually one of the men in white robes came up to me. The fact that my legs were strapped out in front of me on the operating table didn't seem to hinder his ability to stand directly in front of me. As he drew near I felt an overwhelming love radiating from him. I could not see his face, but I could feel how much he cared for me. He reached forward—I could see his arms—and placed his hands on my upper arms.

Though I could not hear words, the message he had for me came clearly into my mind. It was not time for me to go. I still had a lot to do in the physical world.

Though I didn't want to go back, the being in front of me pushed me gently, but firmly, back into my body. I didn't resist his power. I had a great desire to please this man and return to my life here.

The next thing I remember was waking up in my room. I spent two more weeks in the hospital and another six months recovering at home. During that time I was in kind of a haze, with a weird, detached feeling, almost like part of my spirit was not in my body, but that feeling gradually went away.

The operation was a success. The tumor has not returned, though I am still undergoing reconstructive surgery—five operations last year alone. Several years after the operation I served a mission for the LDS Church in Spokane, Washington where I met my wife to be. We live in Utah now where I work for a computer software company. Sometimes life is still hard, but it is good. I am grateful to that man in the white robe who pushed me back into my body.